FROM PLAN TO PANTRY

ORGANIZING A NEIGHBORHOOD FOOD DRIVE

WILLIAM D. HARAZIN

From Plan to Pantry

Previous editions 2020, 2021, 2023

ISBN 978-1-956543-68-1
Printed in the United States of America

Book layout by CSinclaire Write-Design LLC
Cover by Klevur

This book is dedicated to my wife Becky French, who has participated in and supported many food drives and, more importantly, put up with me while I was writing this book.

ACKNOWLEDGMENTS

IN RALEIGH, NORTH Carolina, a young scout named Hardy Weatherspoon was moving up the scouting ranks toward his Eagle Award, which required a service project. Hardy selected a neighborhood food drive as his Eagle Scout Service Project. With the assistance of a few adults, Hardy planned a successful community food drive. That Eagle Scout service project inspired a succession of annual neighborhood food drives that serve as the basis for this book.

A very special thanks goes out to my friend and co-chair, Terry Henderson, who helped guide the process during these food drives.

The 100-plus volunteers of our neighborhood who graciously served as Food Drive Committee Members, Collection Coordinators, and Block Captains—many more than once—all deserve special thanks for their participation in making each of our Neighborhood Food Drives a success. You all know who you are.

CONTENTS

ACKNOWLEDGMENTS v
LIST OF DOCUMENTS. IX
WHERE TO START 1
- Hunger in America. 1
- Why a Food Drive 2
- Sense of Community. 3

NEIGHBORHOOD FOOD DRIVE OVERVIEW 4
- Driven by Local Volunteers 4
- The Plan in a Nutshell 4
- Organizational Structure 5
- Strategy. 6
- Determining the Leadership. 7
- In the Beginning 8

SELECTING THE FOOD BANK BENEFICIARY 9
- Types of Beneficiaries 9
- Communicating with the Food Drive Beneficiary 10

DETERMINING THE FOOD DRIVE'S GEOGRAPHIC NEIGHBORHOOD 13
- Maps 13

DIVIDING THE DESIGNATED NEIGHBORHOOD INTO APPROPRIATE-SIZED BLOCKS 16
- Creating Blocks 16
- Businesses 17

DETERMINING THE TIMELINE OF THE FOOD DRIVE 18
- Timeline 19
- Timing 23

IDENTIFYING POTENTIAL CONTRIBUTORS OF MAPS, GROCERY BAGS, PRINTING, SCALES 25
- Finding Contributors — Grocery Bags and Printing. 25
- Scales 26
- Monetary Donations. 27

RECRUITING BLOCK CAPTAINS AND COLLECTION COORDINATORS 28
- Block Captains 28
- Collection Coordinators. 29
- Recruiting 29
- Block Captain Recruitment 30

Recruiting Collection Coordinators 35
Creating Volunteer Contact Lists 38
Block Assignment List 40

PREPARING THE FLYERS AND OTHER NEIGHBORHOOD COMMUNICATIONS 42
Printables 43
Block Captain Responsibilities 48

PREPARING FOR THE FOOD DRIVE 50
Preparing Block Captain Packages 54
Preparing Collection Coordinator Packages 55
Collection Coordinator Block Captain Bag Package Pick-up 58
Block Captain Bag Delivery 59
Food Bank Volunteers 60
Neighborhood Email Announcing the Food Drive 60
The Reminder Email to Everyone 62

DOCUMENTING THE METRICS OF YOUR FOOD DRIVE 63
Main Metrics 63
Bag Weight Form 65

THE DAY OF THE FOOD DRIVE 69
Neighbors' Bag Delivery 69
Collection Coordinator Bag Pick-up & Delivery 70
Food Bank Set-up 70
Weighing the Bags 71
Completion 72
Publicity 72

COLLECTING STRAGGLER BAGS 74
Straggler Bags Pick-Up & Delivery 74

THANK YOU, THANK YOU, THANK YOU 75
Thank You with Metrics 76

PREPARING FOR CONTINUITY AND SUCCESSION 78

CONCLUSION 79

LIST OF DOCUMENTS

DOCUMENT 1	Kick-Off Email to Food Bank & Donors	83
DOCUMENT 2	Neighborhood Map	84
DOCUMENT 3	Block Captain Recruitment Email	85
DOCUMENT 4	Block Captain Confirmation Email	87
DOCUMENT 5	Block Captain Regrets Email	88
DOCUMENT 6	Collection Coordinator Recruitment Email	89
DOCUMENT 7	Collection Coordinator Confirmation Email	91
DOCUMENT 8	Collection Coordinator Regrets Email	92
DOCUMENT 9	Block Captain Contacts Format	93
DOCUMENT 10	Collection Coordinator Contacts Format	93
DOCUMENT 11	Block Assignment List	94
DOCUMENT 12	Food Drive Flyer	95
DOCUMENT 13	Neighbor Instructions	96
DOCUMENT 14	Block Captain Responsibilities	97
DOCUMENT 15	Block Captain Instructions Email	98
DOCUMENT 16	Collection Coordinator Instructions Email	100
DOCUMENT 17	Bag Count Form	102
DOCUMENT 18	Collection Coordinator Responsibilities.	103
DOCUMENT 19	Announcement of Neighborhood Food Drive Email	104
DOCUMENT 20	Reminder Email to Everyone	105
DOCUMENT 21	Bag Weight Form	106
DOCUMENT 22	Neighbor & Volunteer Thank You Metrics Email	107
DOCUMENT 23	Business Flyer with Metrics	108
DOCUMENT 24	Same-Day Thank You to Volunteers Email	109

— 1 —

WHERE TO START

HUNGER IS USUALLY understood as an uncomfortable or painful sensation caused by insufficient food energy consumption. Scientifically, hunger is referred to as food deprivation according to the Food and Agriculture Organization of the United Nations.[1] According to the *UN Hunger Report*, hunger is the term used to define periods when populations are experiencing severe food insecurity—meaning that they go for entire days without eating due to lack of money, lack of access to food, or other resources.[2]

Hunger in America

When we think of hunger, we generally think of Third World, impoverished nations suffering from war, famine, or catastrophe. But, even in America, the land of the plenty, the hungry exist in significant and intolerable numbers. The number of hungry men, women, and children grew during the coronavirus pandemic and still persists today.

1 http://www.fao.org/hunger/en/

2 State of Food Insecurity and Nutrition in the World 2020 online summary, http://www.fao.org/state-of-food-security-nutrition/en/

The growing number of food insecure Americans is startling, especially considering our country's resources. In September 2024, the USDA released data showing that food insecurity in the United States increased by 6 percent in 2023 and that 47.4 million people—1 in 7 people, including 1 in 5 children—experience food insecurity in the US,[3] the wealthiest nation in the world according to Feeding America.org. This is a lot of hungry people. Whether long term or short term, food insecurity has devastating results physically, mentally, and emotionally on adults and children.

Needs vary from temporary to long term conditions based on individual circumstances such as loss of job, illness, victim of circumstances, or catastrophic event such as a home fire, hurricane, forest fire, flooding, or other catastrophe. Sometimes the condition is obvious. Sometimes it is not. In every city, town, and village there will be people who are food insecure. What can we do to alleviate this? Certainly root causes to wide-spread food insecurity need to be addressed—low wages, economic disruptions, supply chain issues, and more—but in this guide, the focus is on one simple measure to help locally in a timely manner: a neighborhood food drive.

Why a Food Drive

Community-based food relief organizations are dependent on donations and can be strapped to fully meet the needs in their community. Food banks, food pantries, and other charitable organizations too often run short on needed food supplies in general and specific supplies in particular. The plight of children who experience a lack of food in the home worsens when they are deprived of the provided meal or meals they receive at school during the week or when their schools are closed for whatever reasons. Food drives can help fill depleted pantries and provide timely resources to those in need.

3 https://frac.org/news/usdafoodsecurityreportsept2024

Sense of Community

Communities often pull together when tragedy strikes. Whenever there is a disaster or catastrophic event, there is an outpouring of sympathy and a desire to do something to help alleviate the very visible need. Many people will travel to give physical help. Others send money or donate goods to various charitable organizations to help outside their own community. They then look for other ways to assist closer to home. Many don't have a clue on other ways to help, or they feel one person doing something isn't enough to make a difference. **A local food drive is about making a difference by engaging a community to collectively take action in a way that most certainly will make a real, personal difference in lives.**

— 2 —

NEIGHBORHOOD FOOD DRIVE OVERVIEW

Driven by Local Volunteers

The food drive method we use in our community's annual food drive is volunteer driven within a neighborhood and is a simple matter of delegation. **The overarching idea is that if we all do a little, we can accomplish a lot.**

The Plan in a Nutshell

Select the neighborhood area. Divide that area into manageable units that I call "blocks" of approximately 15 homes. Recruit a neighbor within each block as the Block Captain for that block. Recruit sufficient neighbor Collection Coordinators for one to every three to six Block Captains. Obtain the grocery bags and print instructional food drive flyers to be delivered to neighbors a week before the food drive date. Collection Coordinators deliver grocery bags, instructions, and flyers to their assigned Block Captains, who in turn deliver the grocery bags, instructions, and the flyers to the homes within their assigned blocks.

On or before the food drive day, the neighbors, per the instructions provided, will fill their grocery bags and deliver them to their assigned Block Captain's porch. The Collection Coordinators will then pick up the grocery bags from their assigned Block Captains' porches and deliver them to the chosen food bank. Upon delivery, the grocery bags will be counted, weighed, and recorded by volunteers. The next day the Collection Coordinators will pick up straggler bags, if any, from their assigned Block Captains' porches and deliver them to the designated location. Other than sending the appropriate thank you messages, compiling the metrics, and creating after-event publicity, the food drive is successfully completed at this point.

In other words:

- Divide the neighborhood into smaller geographical units or blocks

- Recruit a **Block Captain** volunteer within each geographical block and a **Collection Coordinator** volunteer for a manageable group (3 to 6) of **Block Captains**

- Provide **Collection Coordinators** with flyers and grocery bags for their **Block Captains** to distribute to their group of **Neighbors**

- On the specified collection date, **Neighbors** deliver the filled bags to their Block Captain's porch.

- On the specified collection date, **Collection Coordinators** pick up and deliver the filled bags to the designated food pantry.

Organizational Structure

The simple graphic below shows the recommended structure for enlisting the volunteers needed for this method of collecting food to feed others in the community. More specifics on the responsibilities for these identified volunteers will be presented in later chapters.

— Volunteer Structure —

Volunteer Committee
(provide strategy and oversight of the project)
|
Collection Coordinators
(coordinate and support the efforts of the Block Captains)
|
Block Captains
(work directly with the neighbors for donation collection)
|
Neighbors
(generous people without whom there would be no food drive)

Strategy

Once the idea of a food drive strikes you, plans need to be made and a strategy needs to be devised to carry it out. Whether it is just you or you enlist a couple of neighborhood leaders, the starting point is planning the initial steps to achieve the collection of food.

The first key strategic decision is to determine the leadership for the food drive. From there the following decisions need to be made during the planning stage:

- Select the food pantry(s) to benefit from the food drive
- Determine the area or neighborhood to be covered by the food drive

- Divide the covered neighborhood into appropriate-sized units or "blocks"
- Determine the timeline of the food drive
- Identify and recruit potential contributors of grocery bags, maps, scales, printing
- Identify and recruit Block Captains
- Identify and recruit Collection Coordinators
- Prepare the flyers and other neighborhood communication
- Determine the metrics to be reported for the successful food drive
- Carry out the drive!

Determining the Leadership

The first step is to determine if you are going to lead the food drive by yourself or if you are going to form a volunteer neighborhood committee. The larger the project, the more planning and oversight will be required and the more volunteers needed. Keep in mind, the larger the committee, the more difficult it may be to accommodate schedules in busy lives.

Having a committee can reduce the planning and workload by spreading the responsibilities. Most of the committee work is planning, recruiting volunteers, and "oiling" the food drive machinery during the food drive itself. A small or modest size committee can be agile in getting work done. If you determine it will be a neighborhood committee, keep the size manageable.

Having a committee has advantages, but have a leader who can make decisions, since it may be difficult to obtain consensus at critical times.

Once you have decided the form of leadership, you can move on to the planning.

In the Beginning

In our neighborhood, a young scout selected a neighborhood food drive as his Eagle Award service project. He organized the neighborhood, resulting in a successful food drive that collected nearly 4,000 lbs. of food. Though the food drive was a success, it was also a "one and done" project with no continuity plan.

In 2020, many people were economically suffering during the pandemic, mainly through no fault of their own. With news of people going hungry across the country, I remembered the prior food drive and thought, *Wouldn't a food drive be a good way to help out here in our community?* I mentioned the idea of revisiting the food drive to a friend who had helped organize the 2018 campaign. I was hoping he would take the idea and run with it.

I couldn't have been more wrong. His response was an immediate, "Let's do it." So, he and I became the neighborhood food drive committee planning a food drive. This committee of two worked very well for us as it was relatively easy to get consensus on issues and be nimble enough to quickly take on the various tasks, make quick decisions, find time to meet, and stay on the timeline. This might be more complicated with a larger committee. Nonetheless, whether it's one or two leaders or a committee, large or small, the goal can be accomplished by everyone working together.

— 3 —

SELECTING THE FOOD BANK BENEFICIARY

CHOOSING THE BENEFICIARY of the food drive is one of the first decisions to be made. In determining the beneficiary, keep in mind people are drawn to help organizations they have an affinity to or that they recognize for doing good work in the community. This applies likewise to people who contribute to charitable efforts. Identifying the beneficiary of your food drive should be a significant part of your marketing efforts to promote the drive.

Types of Beneficiaries

The beneficiary of the food drive is generally a charitable organization in your community that distributes food to the homeless, the poor, and the hungry, old and young. They usually go by designations such as food bank, food kitchen, or food pantry. They are generally run by churches, non-profit organizations, or community or government-sponsored entities. Some are large commercial organizations that take large donations of extra food from restaurants and grocery stores. Others are food pantries run by churches or smaller non-profit organizations as a part of their community outreach.

A quick internet search of food banks, food kitchens, or food pantries should result in a number of possible beneficiaries within your community. Checking with local churches, civic clubs, or your local government will also provide you with a list of potential beneficiaries. It will be up to your food drive leadership to select one (or more) of the multiple possible beneficiaries of the food drive. Selection may be determined based on the beneficiary's mission statement, their current needs, or their target constituency as well as where the food drive leadership believes the most impact within their community can be made.

We selected two food banks because in the 2018 food drive more food was collected than the initial food pantry could handle. We selected a church food pantry and an urban ministry that was a large non-profit organization supplied mainly by the commercial grocery store and restaurant food overflow. We felt the church food pantry was the type of smaller organization where our contribution would have an immediate impact. We directed delivery of all of our grocery bags to that location until it was full, and then directed the rest of the grocery bags to the urban ministry program, which could easily handle any contributions we could make. In subsequent years, we selected a small food bank to replace the larger organizational food bank, as again we felt that would have a larger immediate impact on the local community needs.

Communicating with the Food Drive Beneficiary

Once a beneficiary is selected, it is essential that you communicate with them to make sure they don't have any conflicts, that everyone agrees on the times and date of the drive, and that they have sufficient volunteers that day to receive, catalogue, and shelve the food. In working with our two food bank beneficiaries, we found we had to make special arrangements with one since its employees often didn't work on weekends. The smaller food banks usually are run by volunteers whose schedules are more flexible and accommodating.

Though I have provided a list of food items typically needed by the food banks on a sample flyer, most food banks will have their own policies and procedures for receiving donations and their own list of needed items. The food banks generally will also identify those items they cannot/do not receive. You should incorporate the designated food bank's list into the Food Drive Flyer and Neighbor Instructions that will be provided to each neighborhood home.

You will want to know that the food bank will have available volunteers on the day of the food drive to assist in receiving, moving, separating, and shelving the food from the delivery point to the shelves of the food bank. You will also want to determine if the food bank has the necessary supplies and equipment to receive the grocery bags or if the food drive committee will need to provide them. Supplies needed, for example, include a couple of folding tables, 2 to 4 chairs, covered area or tent, scales for weighing the bags, and perhaps water, beverages, or snacks for all of the volunteers.

As you move forward with planning the food drive, you might want to send a Kick Off email to let the beneficiary and supply donors know that plans are underway (Document 1).

— DOCUMENT 1 —

KICK-OFF EMAIL TO FOOD BANK & DONORS

Subject: May 4 Food Drive

All,

We just wanted to let you know we have kicked off our 2024 Food Drive scheduled for May 4 by sending out our Block Captain Recruitment Letter and reaching out to Collection Coordinator volunteers. The recruitment letter below explains the timing and the nuts and bolts of the food drive. We expect to begin bringing the bags of groceries to the food pantry after 1:00 pm on May 4.

We expect the process of delivery, weighing, and receiving the groceries to take no more than two to three hours.

Thank you to those who are donating supplies for the drive. We sincerely appreciate your willingness to do this.

Thanks to all of you for your help and support. If you have any questions, please do not hesitate to call ____________.

Food Drive Committee

(add committee names and contact information)

— 4 —

DETERMINING THE FOOD DRIVE'S GEOGRAPHIC NEIGHBORHOOD

HOW AMBITIOUS YOU are may determine the geographic scope of the food drive. One of the first steps is to determine the geographic boundaries for the food drive and thus the number of participating homes. Looking at city maps will help visualize the area and its breadth. We used the geographic area that essentially was our defined neighborhood. This covered approximately 550 homes in 36 blocks, bounded by 4 major roads.

In 2022, it was discovered that historically, the actual neighborhood boundaries included an adjacent area, so we decided to include that area in the next food drive. This expansion included an additional 10 blocks and approximately 200 homes, thereby expanding our boundaries to include a total of 46 blocks and about 750 homes. *In other words, your boundaries could change for future drives if your neighborhood grows or shrinks.*

Maps

You will need to obtain a detailed neighborhood map that identifies lots and addresses of the homes within the geographic boundaries you identify for your food drive. If your map does not show the addresses, you will need to label the addresses within the geographic boundaries yourself as you will need specific addresses to assign to your volunteers.

Maps can be found in a number of places. Your town, city, or municipality is the best place to start looking since they often have official detailed maps of different defined neighborhoods. Many of these resources are on the government websites of your community. Commercial architecture printers in your area may have maps or can enlarge a smaller map you may have obtained. Doing a Google search may also lead you to suitable maps. It is preferable to have a large map around 2 or 3 feet x 5 feet to make it easy to read the addresses and see the boundary lines of the "blocks" you will create within the neighborhood.

Once you have a detailed map with lots, addresses, and possibly house outlines, you will then have the number of homes within your geographic boundaries. If you cannot find a map with addresses, it may require walking the area to obtain all of the addresses including duplexes, granny flats, and apartment buildings. Even if you do have a detailed map with lots and addresses, you still may want to walk the neighborhood to see if there are unaccounted residential units that will add to the number of homes.

Document 2 following is a copy of the map we used in one of our drives. Though it is hard to see on the map image, we had to pencil in the addresses since our map only showed the lots and the structure outlines. The addresses are important because they give you a good house count to do your planning and because you need them to identify the specific addresses composing each "block" within the geographic neighborhood. Once identified, the addresses will be supplied later to the Block Captains and the Collection Coordinators so they will know their particular area of responsibility within the neighborhood.

We find these assigned addresses may or may not correspond to an actual neighborhood block. The designated blocks for the purpose of the food drive may be up one side and down the other of the street or they may be the addresses on that particular physical block. Or the block may be a different arrangement due to dead ends, Ts in the road, cul de sacs, or multi-family units. The important consideration is being able to make specific assignment of addresses to a particular Block Captain in order to prevent duplication of effort and confusion among the neighbors on where to deliver their filled bags on the food drive day.

— DOCUMENT 2 —

NEIGHBORHOOD MAP

— 5 —

DIVIDING THE DESIGNATED NEIGHBORHOOD INTO APPROPRIATE-SIZED BLOCKS

THE GEOGRAPHIC NEIGHBORHOOD must be split up into manageable "blocks" which, as noted, may or may not correspond to the actual blocks in the neighborhood. In our initial food drive, we had 36 blocks that happened to roughly (but not completely) corresponded to the actual blocks in the neighborhood. There is a twofold reason for not having blocks correspond identically to the actual blocks of the neighborhood. First, each block should have roughly the same number of homes to keep the work evenly distributed for the volunteers, and second, we want to make it as easy as possible for distribution, delivery, and bag collection. Once again, **the overarching idea is that if we all do a little, we can accomplish a lot.**

Creating Blocks

In our experience, the manageable and target number of homes within a block is 15 homes per block within a range of 10 to 20 homes per block. Since Block Captains will be delivering the empty grocery bags to their assigned block and the neighbors within that block will be delivering filled grocery bags to their designated Block Captain's porch, we work to make it simple and easy. For instance, as noted earlier, a designated block may consist of both sides of the street as opposed to the houses on the front, back, and sides of the actual block in order to make the drop-off point (Block Captain's Porch) closer to all of the assigned neighbors in that block.

With a target number of 15 homes per block, the number of homes is divided by 15 to come up with the number of blocks to be designated within the geographic neighborhood. With a target of 15 homes per block with a minimum of 10 and maximum of 20 homes within any one block, the boundary lines of each designated block are able to be drawn. Once the lines are drawn, each block is assigned a block number. We labeled dime-sized, colored stickers to mark each of our created blocks, as shown on our map (Document 2).

Businesses

Though it can be done, we did not initially include businesses in our block numbers. We later included the businesses and, due to their limited number and their concentration in a specific area, we designated them as one block. If businesses are to be counted, each business may have to be designated as their own block since most businesses would probably seek grocery donations from their employees and possibly their customers. Across the business, its employees, and its customers, the target 15 grocery bags might be collected within the business itself.

From our experience, however, we found that very few bags were collected from the businesses within the business block and, in our case, was probably not worth the effort. However, that is not to say that businesses should not be included in helping with the drive. To the contrary, there are other methods of participation and partnership for the businesses, especially by advertising the food drive at their business premises to their customers, thereby creating more awareness within the community.

— 6 —

DETERMINING THE TIMELINE OF THE FOOD DRIVE

IT IS IMPORTANT to the success of the drive to establish a manageable timeline for accomplishing the needed step-by-step tasks. It makes the food drive run smoothly if the planning and the timeline are done at the front end of the process. By breaking down the food drive into tasks and activities and then putting each task and activity on the timeline early in the planning stage, the food drive tasks become manageable and then can be easily delegated.

Our 2020 food drive's timeline was overly aggressive. Of course, this was done while we were self-isolating at home during the coronavirus pandemic and we had lots of time on our hands. After identifying all of the tasks and looking at the time reasonably necessary to accomplish the tasks, we changed our timeline to 28 days from beginning to end. There are some action items that may need either to be decided before the timeline is set or the timeline should be extended to accomplish those early tasks. For example, it takes time to select the food drive beneficiary and determine a mutually convenient food drive date so as not to conflict with holidays, graduation dates, or other neighborhood events. Likewise, defining the neighborhood blocks also takes some time. These things might be decided before the timeline starts or become part of an extended timeline.

Your first food drive will, in all likelihood, need a longer timeline since defining the initial geographic block units, designing suitable flyers, and creating the letters for the first time will take additional time. However, keeping editable copies of your first-year items will make any ensuing years a breeze. The strategy is to reuse your editable first-year items by initially designing or drafting all of your items with this reuse in mind. In doing so, little will need to be changed in future years, other than the food drive date, saving time and energy.

Timeline

Our 28-day timeline with the identified tasks was as follows:

Pre-Day 1 ***Initial Decisions***

- Timeline
- Select and coordinate with food banks
- Determine mutually convenient food drive date
- Define geographic area and unit blocks

Day 1-7 ***Plan Strategy***

- Confirm food bank(s) & date and availability
- Prepare or update Food Drive Flyer (Document 12)
- Prepare or update Neighbor Instructions flyer (Document 13)
- Prepare or update Announcement of Neighborhood Food Drive email (Document 19)
- Prepare or update Block Captain Recruitment email (Document 3)
- Prepare or update Block Captain Confirmation email (Document 4)

- Prepare or update Block Captain Regrets email (Document 5)
- Prepare or update Collection Coordinator Recruitment email (Document 6)
- Prepare or update Collection Coordinator Confirmation email (Document 7)
- Prepare or update Collection Coordinator Regrets email (Document 8)
- Arrange for the purchase or donation of grocery bags
- Determine metrics to collect: # bags, pounds of groceries, # volunteers
- Locate and/or purchase scales
- Create Block Assignment List of Block Captains & Collection Coordinators (Document 11)

Day 8-12 ***Recruitment & Supplies***

- Obtain grocery bags
- Recruit one Block Captain for each block by email & knocking on doors; explain duties
    - Bag delivery to block
    - Receive filled bags from neighbors on food drive day
    - Bring indoors if rain is predicted
- Recruit Group of Collection Coordinators (preferably one for every 3 to 6 Block Captains)
    - Pick up Block Captains Bag Packages from central location
    - Deliver Block Captains' bags to Block Captains
    - Pick up bags from Block Captains' porches on event day
    - Deliver bags to food bank

- Turn in completed Bag Count Form
- Assist in moving bags to the weigh-in area (optional)

- Print Food Drive Flyer & Neighbor Instructions (on one page, front and back) to correspond with the number of homes plus extra (Documents 12, 13)

Day 13-18 ***Assignments***

- Assign blocks & Block Captains to Collection Coordinators (Document 11)
- Designate one Block Captain's porch as the drop off for non-neighborhood donors (optional)
- Assemble appropriate number of bags, flyers, responsibilities sheet, and block addresses into Bag Packages for each Block Captain (Documents 11, 12, 13, 14)
- Assemble Collection Coordinators' assigned Block Captain Bag Packages into stacks (possibly with student volunteers)
- Add Collection Coordinator Block Assignment List showing their Block Captain information, a Bag Count Form, and a Responsibilities sheet (Documents 11, 17, 18)
- Collection Coordinators pick up Bag Packages from central location about 7 days prior to food drive day
- Email Block Captain Instructions (Document 15)
- Email Collection Coordinator Instructions (Document 16)
- Obtain 1 or 2 scales for bag weighing

Day 19-22 ***Reminder Emails***

- Email flyers to neighbors, if possible (Document 20)
- Email reminder to Block Captains with instructions (Document 20)
- Email reminder to Collection Coordinators with instructions (Document 20)

Day 23 ***Food Drive Day***

- Neighbors deliver grocery bags to their Block Captain's porch by 1:00 pm on drive day
- Collection Coordinators pick-up bags from Block Captains starting at 1:00 pm
- Collection Coordinators deliver bags to food banks between 1:00 – 3:00 pm
- Bags are weighed & recorded when they are delivered to food bank (Document 21)
- Collection Coordinators turn in completed Bag Count Form (Document 17)
- Photos of volunteers can be taken during the delivery and weighing process
- Same Day Thank You email is sent to Block Captains, Collection Coordinators, volunteers, and the food bank after food drive is complete (Document 24)
- Collection Coordinators sent a reminder email to check for straggler bags

Day 24 ***Pick-up of Straggler Bags***

- Collection Coordinators pick-up straggler bags from Block Captains porches
- Collection Coordinators deliver straggler bags to designated location

Day 25 ***Delivery of Straggler Bags***

- Deliver straggler bags to Food Bank

Day 26 ***Prepare and send Neighbor & Volunteer Thank You & Metrics message***

- Prepare metrics message to share (Document 22)

Day 28 ***Business Flyer with Metrics Thank You***

- Prepare flyer with metrics and thanks to post in businesses (Document 23)
- Recognition of Collection Coordinators, Captains, donors, and food banks
- Publicity

Timing

In our experience, the best time to have a food drive is on a Saturday when most volunteers are not working. We scheduled the 2020 food drive on Memorial Day weekend, because we wanted to do it as soon as possible and thought that most families would be staying home due to COVID-19. However, we found that a significant number of families were out of town. As such, based on our experience, it is recommended to have the food drive on a weekend other than a holiday, graduation date, significant sports event, or hunting season opening day. That being said, we thought that it might be a good idea to have the food drive on a Saturday close to a holiday so that the holiday could be used as a theme for the food drive.

In selecting a specific date for your drive, check with your community and the intended beneficiary food bank to see if there is any conflict with the date. Other groups, churches, or organizations may already be planning a food drive targeting your area. The U.S. Postal Service has a large national food drive initiative in the spring of each year. It is best to avoid dates with competing food drives or similar events or initiatives. The intended beneficiary food bank may also have conflicts. As the receiving party, the intended beneficiary food bank generally needs to know you are coming and needs to have ready their own volunteers to receive, catalogue, and shelve the food. As such, coordination of the date with the intended beneficiary food bank is essential.

In addition to the foregoing concerns in selecting a date, keep in mind that the food drive is essentially two weekends in a row. The weekend prior to the food drive date is the weekend that the Collection Coordinators deliver the empty grocery bags to the Block Captains, who in turn will deliver the bags to their neighbors, preferably during that same weekend prior to the food drive. This week allows enough time for the neighbors to fill the bags in preparation for the day of the food drive. Although not as labor intensive as the date of the food drive, the weekend prior to the food drive should also avoid holidays, graduations and other potential conflicts. We have found the last couple of weeks of April or early May often are good dates that fall between Easter and graduations and other potential conflicts.

Once a drive day is selected, the above timeline can easily be adapted for your drive by backing up the timeline dates from the selected date for the event.

— 7 —

IDENTIFYING POTENTIAL CONTRIBUTORS OF MAPS, GROCERY BAGS, PRINTING, SCALES

PEOPLE GENERALLY WANT to help a good cause and often they will do so if you just ask. The food drive's largest physical needs, other than volunteers, are maps, grocery bags, printing, and a scale or two. Most of the other needs fall under volunteer labor for the planning, bag distribution, bag collection, and bag delivery.

Finding Contributors — Grocery Bags and Printing

Chapter 3 provided information on ways to find maps for your neighborhood. You may find an organization, church, or group of individuals willing to donate the number of grocery bags you need. Grocery bags can be purchased easily in bulk from commercial paper suppliers, such as Uline (uline.com) or other major suppliers. The bags are relatively inexpensive. According to the 2024 Uline catalogue, 300 bags cost about $92.00.

In reviewing the material from an earlier food drive, we found that the outreach division of a local church had donated 750 bags. We reached out to them, and they were more than happy to participate by providing sufficient bags for our 2020 food drive effort and have continued to do so in following drives. There likely are charitable entities in your neighborhood willing to participate "in kind."

Most of the food drive communication in our food drives is done by email or telephone. The big exception is the distribution of the double-sided Food Drive Flyer and Neighbor Instructions. You may want to have that printed by a local printing shop as a two-sided document. The number of copies we printed was between 1½ and 2 times the number of projected homes. In our case, we initially had approximately 550 homes, so we had a local printer print 1,000 copies front and back. We were able to find a donor to pay for the printing, which in 2024 was approximately $150 for 1,000 colored paper copies, front and back. Many printing companies have a daily rotating selected color paper that is discounted or the same price as regular white paper. Printing on color paper gives the flyer more impact.

We considered but did not use a second distribution of the flyer as a reminder of the upcoming drive. We do have several email lists, which we use to email a soft copy of both sides of the flyer to various neighborhood groups as part of the publicity for the food drive.

Scales

Some food banks have commercial scales to weigh the bags of food as they arrive. If not, then a scale or two will need to be located and procured for the date of the food drive if you want to track metrics for your event. We found the church food pantry did not have a scale and the large urban ministry had a large commercial scale to weigh all the bags at one time. Since our first drive, we obtained two donated digital scales, each costing under $50. Two scales could be used simultaneously with two food bank beneficiaries or together at one beneficiary.

Monetary Donations

Since this is a food drive, we do not promote (or discourage) monetary donations, though the preference would be for food donations. We do not speak of monetary donations in any of our flyers, emails, or communications. We address monetary donations only if we are asked. Nonetheless, invariably there are some who wish to make a monetary donation, which we gladly accept.

We do not want to be a banker in this endeavor. As such, we do not accept credit cards or cash. However, we will accept checks payable to the beneficiary of the food drive. Upon conclusion of the food drive, the checks are delivered to the respective food bank. We do keep track of the monetary donations so that they become a part of the food drive metrics.

— 8 —

RECRUITING BLOCK CAPTAINS AND COLLECTION COORDINATORS

I CANNOT STRESS enough the importance of having a plan to identify and recruit both Block Captains and Collection Coordinators, which the leadership should do within the first week. As previously indicated, the first two steps are designating the geographic boundaries of the selected neighborhood and then splitting the geographic neighborhood into manageable blocks, which may or may not correspond to the actual blocks in the neighborhood. As noted earlier, either determine the blocks before your time line starts or allow extra time in your timeline to accomplish this.

Block Captains

The number of Block Captains to recruit depends on and corresponds to the number of block units delineated within the designated neighborhood. For example, if you have 36 block units you would need to recruit 36 Block Captains. Moreover, since the Block Captain's porch becomes the delivery point for the neighbors on that particular block unit, ideally recruit one resident from each block unit. Though not necessary, it is helpful to recruit a Block Captain who has a covered front porch in case of inclement weather.

Collection Coordinators

The number of Collection Coordinators is dependent on the number of Block Captains. On the day of the food drive, a Collection Coordinator will be responsible for collecting the grocery bags from a certain number of assigned Block Captains' front porches. Since we have a limited time to collect the bags and deliver them to the food banks on the day of the food drive, we determined that a manageable group for a Collection Coordinator was between 3 and 6 Block Captains' porches with the preference being 3. So, if you have 36 Block Captains you would need to recruit between 6 and 12 Collection Coordinators.

Once Collection Coordinators have been recruited, then each would be assigned an equal number of Block Captains to whom they would deliver the Block Captain Bag Package with grocery bags and Food Drive Flyer & Neighbor Instructions and from whom they would collect the filled grocery bags on the day of the food drive. In recruiting Collection Coordinators, we avoided recruiting individual neighbors who were already Block Captains where possible, thereby spreading out the work and providing a greater sense of community. Since the designated food drive geographic area is relatively compact and the neighborhood volunteers serving as Collection Coordinators will be driving, there is more latitude in assigning them Block Captain locations.

Recruiting

In recruiting the Block Captains and Collection Coordinators, leadership uses their neighborhood contacts to identify potential volunteers. The Block Captains' main duties are delivering the empty grocery bags with the Food Drive Flyer & Neighbor Instructions and having the neighbors return full grocery bags to their front porch. The Collection Coordinators' primary duties are delivering the Block Captain Bag Packages to their assigned

Block Captains, retrieving the full bags on food drive day, and delivering the bags to the food banks.

Since there is not a lot of work involved in being a Block Captain and just a little bit of sweat for the Collection Coordinators, along with the fact that it's for a good cause, we typically found it relatively easy to recruit the Block Captains and the Collection Coordinators once we were able to identify a potential volunteer. The ask is fairly easy and for a good cause, so it is hard to turn down. Again, if we all do a little, we can accomplish a lot.

Also consider you will need volunteers on the day of the food drive at the food bank to help with unloading and moving the bags of groceries, weighing the bags, and assisting the food bank volunteers. They simply need to arrive at the food bank at the designated time. Certainly, Block Captains and Collection Coordinators can volunteer for this, but other neighbors might also wish to help.

When recruiting volunteers, make sure you obtain or verify contact information, including name, address, telephone number, and email address for use in maintaining a list of Block Captains and Collection Coordinators.

We send a recruitment email to interested volunteers, providing information about the drive and the duties to be performed. After the first drive, you will have a jump on recruiting both Block Captains and Collection Coordinators for future drives, since you will already have a list of email addresses for each group of volunteers. At that point, you can simply send a modified recruitment email to your list, reminding them of their prior service and refresh them on the simple duties of their service.

Block Captain Recruitment

Your recruitment for Block Captains may employ neighborhood connections, referrals, and telephone recruitment. Follow up initial contact with an email or make a Block Captain Recruitment email your first contact to verify information about the event, the beneficiary, and the volunteer's duties. (Document 3) For those who agreed to be a Block Captain, we send a follow-up Confirmation email (Document 4), or, if they were unable to be a Block Captain, we send a Regrets email (Document 5) asking for their help in finding a Captain for their block.

The large neighborhood map with the block units delineated and numbered is also very useful in identifying blocks that need a Block Captain as we continue recruiting. When we identify a block that still needs a Block Captain, we put a yellow sticky note or pin on the map for that block, making it quickly identifiable. Then we fall back on our neighborhood contacts to fill most of the openings. For the last few to be filled, we walk the streets of the specific blocks needing a Block Captain. We look for neighbors working in their yards, and we knock on doors. We look for homes with covered porches to serve as a collection point in case of inclement weather. The "ask" is not big, and we only have to approach one or two neighbors on any particular block to find a volunteer. When the Block Captain is recruited, we remove the note or pin from the map, so we can always see at a glance if any block needs a Captain.

— DOCUMENT 3 —

BLOCK CAPTAIN RECRUITMENT EMAIL

Subject: Request for volunteers for Neighborhood Food Drive

Several of us in the neighborhood are spearheading a Neighborhood Food Drive to help address the needs of the hungry and food insecure in our community. Food insecurity in the United States increased by 6% in 2023. It is reported that 47.4 million people—1 in 7 people, including 1 in 5 children—experience food insecurity in the US. Even here in our community there is food insecurity. We will be collecting food for a local food bank to help them achieve their mission of meeting the needs of the hungry in our community. **A local food drive is about making a difference by engaging a community to collectively take action in a way that most certainly will make a real, personal difference in lives.** We are asking you to be a Block Captain for the Neighborhood Food Drive Campaign. It will be so easy to participate.

Here's how:

The Neighborhood Food Drive is Saturday, May 4, 2024

1. You will be assigned to represent about 10 to 15 houses on your block area.
2. **Around April 27**, you will receive a package of empty grocery bags from one of your neighbors, who has agreed to assist in the coordination of the food collection. You will receive flyers with suggestions for food to contribute and instructions on returning the bags full of groceries to your front porch on **Saturday, May 4 before 1:00 pm.** Finally, you will receive a list of addresses on or around your home for grocery bag distribution.
3. As soon as possible after receipt of the grocery bags and the flyers, **print your name and address on the flyer so neighbors will know where to drop off their groceries**. Staple or tape a flyer to the outside of each grocery bag so your name is showing. Then the bags should be distributed right away to your neighbors *at the addresses assigned to you.*
4. **On Saturday, May 4, before 1:00 pm**, your assigned neighbors will drop off their filled grocery bags to your front porch. You need not be present. If there are any straggler bags, please call your Collection Coordinator ASAP so they can be picked up during the Food Drive. Otherwise, they will be picked up on Sunday, **May 5.**
5. **On Saturday, May 4, after 1:00 pm,** your Collection Coordinator will pick up the grocery bags from your front porch and take them to the food bank. You need not be present.

6. On **Sunday, May 5, after 1:00 pm**, your Collection Coordinator will pick up from your front porch any grocery bags from any stragglers who missed the deadline and take them to the designated location. You need not be present.
7. If you also want to assist in the loading, unloading and delivery of the grocery bags for the food bank, we certainly could use the assistance to make this food drive a success.

With everyone doing a little, we will accomplish a lot. **Please confirm by return email (with your telephone number and address) that you will be a Food Drive Block Captain**. This is one small way we can all help.

If for any reason you will be unable to serve as a Block Captain, would you please help us find your replacement by quickly recruiting a neighbor on your block and let us know the individual's contact information? Many thanks for your consideration.

Food Drive Committee

(add committee names and contact information)

— DOCUMENT 4 —

BLOCK CAPTAIN CONFIRMATION EMAIL

Subject: Thank you for volunteering to help with the Neighborhood Food Drive

Thank you so much for volunteering to be a Block Captain for the 2024 Neighborhood Food Drive. With your help, we can do a lot to help out those who are in need.

You will receive the grocery bags along with a two-side event flyer & instructions for the homes on your assigned block about a week before the Saturday, May 4 Food Drive Day. You will need to put your name and address on the instruction side of the flyer, attach that flyer to each bag (instruction side facing out) and then deliver the bags to the homes on your assigned block. If you have any homes on your block that are not listed, please deliver bags to the unlisted homes and let us know the addresses so we can add them to the list for future drives.

On Saturday, May 4, the neighbors on your block will return the filled grocery bags to your front porch (covered area in the event of inclement weather) by 1:00 pm and soon thereafter the Collection Coordinators will come by and pick up all the bags. If neighbors drop off bags late, let your Collection Coordinator know, and the bags will either be picked up later on drive day or the next day.

Again, thanks so much for volunteering!

Food Drive Committee

(Add member names and contact information)

— DOCUMENT 5 —

Block Captain Regrets Email

Subject: May we ask for your help?

Thank you for your response. We are sorry, as we know you are, that you will be unable to volunteer as a Block Captain for our Neighborhood Food Drive.

Is it possible for you to recruit one of your neighbors to be a Block Captain or can you suggest someone in the neighborhood that we might approach to be a Block Captain? Since time is important, please let us know at your earliest convenience.

Thanks for your consideration and your continued support of this project.

Food Drive Committee

(Add member names and contact information)

Recruiting Collection Coordinators

During our initial food drive, a number of older Scouts served as the Collection Coordinators. We did not have the scout's names or email addresses, and, in all likelihood, most had aged out of Scouting. As such, we started from scratch identifying potential volunteers for Collection Coordinators from our own neighborhood contacts. Alternatively, we could have contacted the local Boy Scout Troop, Girl Scout Troop, or other community group to see if they needed a service project. Once we identify and verbally recruit a Collection Coordinator and obtain their contact information, we send them a Collection Coordinator Recruitment email that verifies the event information and lists Collection Coordinators' duties (Document 6).

We send a Collection Coordinator Confirmation email (Document 7) to those who accept, and for those who cannot accept, we send a Collection Coordinator Regrets email (Document 8) and ask for their help recruiting a replacement Collection Coordinator.

— DOCUMENT 6 —

COLLECTION COORDINATOR RECRUITMENT EMAIL

Subject: Request for volunteers for Neighborhood Food Drive

The Neighborhood Food Drive Committee is spearheading a Neighborhood Food Drive to help address the needs of the hungry and food insecure in our community. Food insecurity in the United States increased by 6% in 2023. It is reported that 47.4 million people—1 in 7 people, including 1 in 5 children—experience food insecurity in the US. Even here in our community. We will be collecting food for a local food bank to help them achieve their mission of meeting the needs of the hungry in our community. **A local food drive is about making a difference by engaging**

a community to collectively take action in a way that most certainly will make a real, personal difference in lives.

We are asking you to be a Collection Coordinator for this Neighborhood Food Drive on **Saturday, May 4**. It will be so easy to participate.

As a Coordinator, you will be assigned a small number of volunteer Block Captains. We intend and expect to have 48 Block Captains, and you will likely be the coordinator for 3 of them. The Committee is in the process of signing up the Block Captains. Once this is accomplished, we will let you know which ones would be assigned to you.

We will be sending you more details for your role in the food drive shortly, but simply, your duties will be:

1. Picking up a set of grocery bags and flyers with instructions for each of your Block Captains from a designated location between **April 25-27** from 10:00 am - 6:00 pm
2. Delivering the grocery bags and flyers with instructions to each of your Block Captains
3. Responding to any questions from the Block Captains or referring them to a Food Drive Committee member
4. On Saturday, **May 4**, beginning at 1:00 pm, picking up the bags of food from the front porch of each of your Block Captains
5. Counting the bags for each Block Captain and entering the count on the Bag Count Form
6. Delivering the bags of food to the designated Food Bank
7. On Sunday **May 5**, picking up any straggler bags of food from each of your Block Captains' front porches
8. Delivering straggler bags to designated collection point

With everyone doing a little, we will accomplish a lot. **Please confirm by return email (with your telephone number and address) if you will be a Neighborhood Food Drive Collection Coordinator this year.**

If for any reason, you will be unable to serve as a Collection Coordinator, as time is of the essence, please help us find your replacement by recruiting a neighbor and letting us know the individual's contact information or simply share a name and we will make the contact.

Many thanks for your consideration. This is one small way we can all help.

In the meantime, if you have questions, feel free to reach out to us.

Neighborhood Food Drive Committee

(add committee names and contact information)

— DOCUMENT 7 —

COLLECTION COORDINATOR CONFIRMATION EMAIL

Subject: Thank you for volunteering to help with the Neighborhood Food Drive

Thank you so much for volunteering to be a Collection Coordinator for the 2024 Neighborhood Food Drive. With your help we can do a lot to help out those who are in need.

You will be able to pick up sets of bags and flyers to deliver to your Block Captains on ____________ between _________ at ____________. We ask that the set of bags and flyers be delivered to your Block Captains as soon as possible so they can be distributed timely to the homes on their respective blocks. Then on May 4 starting at 1:00 pm, please pick up the filled bags from the porch of each of your Block Captains and deliver them to our designated food bank. On May 5, please check the porches of your Block Captains again to see if there are any straggler bags and, if so, deliver them to the designated location.

Again, thanks so much for volunteering!

Food Drive Committee

(Add member names and contact information)

— DOCUMENT 8 —

Collection Coordinator Regrets Email

Subject: May we ask for your help?

Thank you for your response. We are sorry, as we know you are, that you will be unable to volunteer as Collection Coordinator for our Neighborhood Food Drive.

Is it possible for you to recruit one of your neighbors to be a Collection Coordinator or can you suggest someone in the neighborhood that we might approach to be a Collection Coordinator? Since time is important, please let us know at your earliest convenience.

Thanks for your consideration and your continued support of this project.

Food Drive Committee

(Add member names and contact information)

Creating Volunteer Contact Lists

Once recruitment starts, we make an email group contact list of the Block Captain contacts, including name, home address, telephone number, email address, block number, and whether they committed with a yes or responded no. We use a work address field to put the block number into the email contact list. This allows us to easily see the blocks still needing Block Captains and allows us to efficiently update the list as needed.

An example for a Block Captain Contact (Document 9) is set out below. Notice the work address holds the Block Captain's block number since we didn't need a Block Captain's work address. If we had needed it, we could have created a third address for the work address.

On the Collection Coordinator Contact (Document 10) instead of entering the block number in the work field, we included the assigned block numbers with the last name of its associated Block Captain.

— DOCUMENT 9 —

Block Captain Contacts Format

NAME	CONTACT INFO	PHONE
John Q. Public	johnq@gmail.com HOME: 1234 Main Street Sometown, NC 99999 WORK: Block 12 - Yes	919-999-9999 (cell)

— DOCUMENT 10 —

Collection Coordinator Contacts Format

NAME	CONTACT INFO	PHONE
John Q. Public	johnq@gmail.com HOME: 1234 Main Street Sometown, NC 99999 WORK: Block 12 - Smith Block 15 - Jones Block 16 - Brown	919-999-9999 (cell)

We also did lists for the supply donors, food bank contacts and for general volunteers, thereby having separate email contact groups for easy reference across our interested parties.

As with any project involving volunteers, circumstances can and do change. During the weeks leading up to the food drive date, we lost a few volunteers to family or other conflicts, which required us to recruit new volunteers. When this occurred, we would ask them for their help recruiting their replacement. The email contact lists allowed us to keep up with these change in circumstances.

Block Assignment List

As you begin recruiting Block Captains, build a Block Assignment List of all the designated blocks and fill in the names of the Block Captains as they volunteer for a particular block. Then once you identify volunteers for Collection Coordinators, you can add their names to the Block Assignment List (Document 11). That list will identify:

- Blocks in numerical order
- Number of bags needed for each specific block
- Name of Collection Coordinator
- Name of Block Captain
- Address of Block Captain
- Addresses on each block where bags are to be delivered by that Block Captain

— DOCUMENT 11 —

Block Assignment List

Block 1 = 16 Bags **Smith** (Collection Coordinator)

Jones (Block Captain) 2113 Cherry St
Block Addresses:
Cherry Street — 2101, 2105, 2107, 2109, 2111, 2113, 2115, 2117, 2123, 2201, 2203, 2207, 2213
Elm Street — 2506, 2508, 2510

Block 2 = 18 Bags **Brown**

Green 2118 Glen St
Block Addresses:
Glen St — 2014, 2108, 2110, 2114, 2116, 2118, 2202, 2204, 2206, 2208, 2210, 2211, 2212, 2214, 2216
Meadow Rd — 2406, 2408, 2410

Block 3 = 14 Bags **Black**

Adams 2130 Washington Dr
Block Addresses:
Washington Dr — 2127, 2128, 2129, 2130, 2131, 2132, 2133, 2134, 2135, 2137, 2139, 2141, 2020, 2022

— 9 —

PREPARING THE FLYERS AND OTHER NEIGHBORHOOD COMMUNICATIONS

CREATING FLYERS, RECRUITMENT letters, instructions, and even the thank you letters from scratch can be daunting. However, the sentiment and content in all are the same. They need to provide the relevant information of who, what, where, when, and how. They also must be plain, simple, and to the point. It is time-saving and helpful to plan and prepare all your communication messages early in the process so there is no last-minute push to craft a message. Once you have determined the major points of the food drive, such as the date, the times, the food bank beneficiary, and their needed items, this information can easily be incorporated into the communication materials. To make it easy for you, I have provided sample communication documents, which can be modified for your specific needs.

If the food drive becomes an annual event, it gets easier because all of the communication materials will only need to be updated with the new information each year. Keeping editable copies of your first-year items will be valuable resources. As mentioned earlier, the strategy is to reuse your editable first-year items by initially designing or drafting all of your items with reuse in mind. This way other than the food drive date, little will need to be changed in future years, saving a lot of time and energy.

Here are possible communications you might prepare.

Printables

Quantity printables

- Food Drive Flyers (Document 12)
- Neighbor Instructions to participate in food drive donations with list of needed grocery items (Document 13)

User printables

- Collection Coordinator Bag Count Form (Document 17)
- Bag Weight Form (Document 21) – one for each weigh-in table

Email Communications

Consider assigning a task to create templates for these messages to have them ready when needed.

- Block Captain Recruitment message (Document 3)
- Collection Coordinator Recruitment message (Document 6)
- Block Captain Confirmation email (Document 4)
- Collection Coordinator Confirmation email (Document 7)
- Block Captain & Collection Coordinator Regrets Email (Documents 5 & 8)
- Block Captain Responsibilities (Document 14)

- Collection Coordinator Responsibilities (Document 18)
- Neighborhood event Announcement and Reminder emails if that is an option (Document 19, 20)
- Neighbor & Volunteer Thank You Metrics (Document 22)
- Business Flyer with metrics to post in businesses (Document 23)
- Press release announcement recognizing volunteers and drive outcome (optional)

Samples for most of these messages can be found throughout these pages and in the appendix of this book.

The Food Drive Flyer

The Food Drive Flyer (Document 12) can be used as a template or an inspiration for creating a flyer modified to your community's special needs. Here are things to consider including in the flyer:

- Identify the neighborhood
- Identify the beneficiary of the drive
- Give the date of the drive
- Identify the ask (food donations)
- Add a brief encouraging message

You might also consider using the same basic flyer information to announce the food drive and give contact information to get more information in a more visible 8.5" x 17" poster to place, with permission, in businesses and other appropriate locations, being careful not to violate any HOA or neighborhood rules.

— DOCUMENT 12 —

FOOD DRIVE FLYER

Who, What, When, Where, Why

A number of us in the neighborhood have recognized the need for a food drive to help out the hungry and food insecure of our community, so the neighborhood is holding a **Neighborhood Food Drive** on May 4, 2024,, and we hope you will support it.

The groceries collected will benefit ____________.

- **Around April 27**, a week before the **May 4** Neighborhood Food Drive, you will receive an empty grocery bag on your doorstep from your neighborhood Food Drive Block Captain with suggestions for items needed by the food bank benefiting from the food drive.
- Please return the bag with the food items to your Block Captain's porch no later than **1:00 pm on May 4**.
- Our goal is to raise over 4,000 pounds of food to help feed the hungry in our area. We hope you will support this project in any way you can.
- **For more information contact:** Food Drive Committee. Email, telephone number

— See reverse for more Food Drive information! —

We also prepare a one-page Neighbor Instruction sheet that includes a list of grocery items needed by the food bank (Document 13). The instruction sheet asks the neighbors to fill a grocery bag and return it to their assigned Block Captain's porch within the time deadline on the date of the food drive so the groceries can be delivered to the food bank or pantry that same day.

— DOCUMENT 13 —

Neighbor Instructions

Neighborhood Food Drive May 4, 2024

Thank you for your participation in the Neighborhood Food Drive! Please return the bag to your Block Captain by **1:00 pm, Saturday, May 4**. If you will be out of town for the weekend, you can return your bag early to your Block Captain.

Your Block Captain is: ______________________________

Address: ______________________________

Most Wanted Food & Grocery Items

- No glass
- Canned pasta with meat (example: ravioli w/ meatballs)
- Beef stew and healthy soups
- Cereal/granola/oatmeal & other breakfast items (all sizes)
- Chicken or tuna (cans or pouches), salmon
- Canned chili with beans and/or black beans
- Mac & cheese (cups or boxes)
- Cliff bars, kind bars, or granola bars
- Individual fruit cups or canned fruit

- Individual vegetable cups or canned vegetables, beans & tomatoes
- Juice boxes
- Sandwich crackers
- Peanut butter and jelly
- Pasta and rice
- Dried peas, beans

— See reverse for more Food Drive information! —

Of course, there were and will be hiccups. Neighbors will call to ask the identity of their Block Captain (even though clearly listed on the instructions) or filled grocery bags might be delivered a day or two before the date of the food drive. We found none of these issues were major or insurmountable. The Block Captains capably dealt with the issues as they arose.

When printing the flyer, consider making the Neighbor Instruction sheet the flip side of the Food Drive Flyer so only one sheet of paper is used, thereby saving a small forest. In our drives, as noted earlier, we print about 1½ to 2 times the number of projected homes and use colored paper to make it stand out ($150 for 1,000 copies front and back in 2024). We also had several email lists that we were able to use to email the flyer itself to various neighborhood groups as part of the publicity for the food drive.

The primary purpose of the Food Drive Flyer & Neighbor Instruction sheet is to attach one to each of the empty grocery bags with the Instruction side facing out to easily identify the Block Captain's name and address. This sheet can be attached to the bags by staple or tape by the respective Block Captain after filling in their name and address to prepare the bags for delivery. Throughout the year, most of us receive sheets of preprinted name and address stickers from various charitable organizations to be used as return addresses on our mail. Some Block Captains use these stickers to put their name and address on the Instruction sheet thereby saving time.

Block Captain Responsibilities

In addition to printing the two-sided sheet flyer with Neighbor Instructions on colored paper, we also had sufficient Block Captain Responsibilities (Document 14) printed for each Block Captain. Typically, we print 1 1/2 times the number of Block Captains. To make them stand out and to distinguish them from the two-sided sheet Food Drive Flyers, we had them printed on a different color paper because these Block Captain Instructions would become a part of the Block Captain packages.

— DOCUMENT 14 —

Block Captain Responsibilities

Block Captain Responsibilities

A Block Captain's main duties are delivering the grocery bags with the Food Drive Flyer & Neighbor Instructions and having the neighbors return the grocery bags to their front porch. More specifically:

- A Block Captain will be assigned 10 to 15 houses in Block Captain's block.
- At least a week prior to the food drive date, a package of empty grocery bags will be delivered to the Block Captain's home along with Food Drive Flyer & Neighbor Instructions and a list of assigned addresses on or around the Block Captain's address.
- Upon receipt, the each flyer should be filled in with the Block Captain's name and address and attached to the outside of a grocery bag, the instruction side facing outward.
- As soon after bag receipt and preparation as possible, the bags should be distributed to the assigned addresses.
- On the food drive date, before 1:00 pm, your assigned neighbors will drop off their full grocery bags to your front porch. You need not be present.

- On the food drive date, after 1:00 pm, the grocery bags will be picked up from your front porch and taken to the food bank. You need not be present.
- The day after the food drive date, after 1:00 pm, any straggler bags that missed the deadline will be picked up and delivered to the designated location. You need not be present.
- If you want to assist in the loading, unloading and delivery of the grocery bags to the food bank, your assistance would be appreciated.

— 10 —

PREPARING FOR THE FOOD DRIVE

NOW THAT THE geographic area has been designated and divided into appropriate block units, one or more food banks have been selected, Block Captains and Collection Coordinators have been recruited, bags, and scales have been obtained, and printed and email documents have been created and printed where necessary, it's time to turn our attention to executing the food drive.

The bags should be distributed throughout the neighborhood the **weekend prior** to the food drive, thereby allowing adequate time for the neighbors to fill the bags for the food drive date the following weekend. The process begins with emailing the Block Captain Instructions and the Collection Coordinators Instructions (Documents 15 & 16) approximately two weeks prior to the Food Drive date. The instruction emails cover the duties already communicated with the Block Captains and the Collection Coordinators in the recruiting process.

— DOCUMENT 15 —

Block Captain Instructions Email

Block Captains!

We have been planning, preparing, and recruiting for the 2024 NEIGHBORHOOD FOOD DRIVE, and we are so thankful for all of you who have volunteered to be a Block Captain. The Food Drive is a worthy way to help those in need.

All of the 2024 planning is complete, and now it's time to execute. Here is your action plan for the Saturday, May 4 Food Drive.

1. During the early part of the weekend of April 27, the Collection Coordinators will drop off at your house sufficient grocery bags (12 to 20) for the assigned houses on your block unit.
2. You will also receive 2-sided flyers with suggestions for food to contribute and instructions on returning the grocery bags to your front porch on Saturday, May 4, before 1:00 pm. A copy of the 2-sided flyer is attached.
3. Last but not least, the Block Assignment List of assigned addresses is attached. Look for your name on the list. Block Captain's name and address are listed in BOLD on the left-hand side under the Block Number. The Collection Coordinator's name is listed in BOLD on the middle across from the Block Number. Look closely at your assigned addresses, which do not necessarily coincide with your own block.
4. Upon receipt, please fill in your name and address on the Neighbor Instructions side of the flyer (Hint: Use the freebie address labels you regularly receive from charitable organizations). The flyer should be stapled or taped to the outside of each grocery bag with your name and address showing outward.
5. Early in the week prior to the food drive, distribute the bags to your neighbors *at the addresses assigned* to you to give them enough time to fill the bags with groceries. Let us know if you need more bags or if there are any omitted addresses on your block area so we can add them to the

list. Look closely at your assigned addresses, which do not necessarily coincide with your exact block.

6. On Saturday, May 4, before 1:00 pm, your assigned neighbors will drop off their full grocery bags on your front porch. You need not be present. If you will have a drop off point other than your front porch, let us know so we will know where to pick up the groceries. We will urge your neighbors to deliver the groceries where possible on the morning of Saturday, May 4. Rain or shine, it will be Saturday, May 4. Please try to protect the bags from the elements in case of inclement weather.
7. On Saturday, May 4 after 1:00 pm, Collection Coordinators will pick up the grocery bags from your front porch and take them to the food bank. You need not be present. Let your Collection Coordinator know ASAP if anyone delivers bags late, so they can be picked up while the food drive is ongoing if possible.
8. On Sunday, May 5, after 1:00 pm, your Collection Coordinator will pick up any straggler bags that missed the deadline and take them to the designated location. You need not be present.
9. If you want to assist in the loading, delivery, and unloading of the grocery bags, we certainly could use the assistance to make this food drive a success.
10. Once we get everything tallied, we will let you know the results of our collection effort.

If you have any questions or run into any issues, please call __________.

Many thanks for your efforts. This is one small way we can all make a difference.

Food Drive Committee

(Add member names and contact information)

— DOCUMENT 16 —

Collection Coordinator Instructions Email

Collection Coordinators!

We have been planning, preparing, and recruiting for the 2024 NEIGHBORHOOD FOOD DRIVE, and we are so thankful for all of you who have volunteered to be a Collection Coordinator. The Food Drive is a worthy way to help out those in need.

All of the food drive planning is done and now it's time to execute. Here is your action plan for the Saturday, May 4 Food Drive.

1. Each of the Collection Coordinators will be assigned 3 Block Captains to whom you will deliver bags and pick up groceries. Your Assigned Block Captains are on the attached Block Assignment List.

2. Between April 25-27, 10:00 am to 6:00 pm, please pick up the assigned Bag Packages with grocery bags, flyers, and a list of assigned addresses for your Block Captains at ____________. Please call or email (999-999-9999 or ___________@gmail.com) to let us know the approximate time you will pick up your three sets of bags or if there are any issues in picking up the bags.

3. As soon as possible after pick-up but in any event by April 27, deliver the appropriate grocery bags, flyers, and list of assigned addresses to your Block Captains and respond to any questions they may have.

4. On Saturday, Saturday, May 4 starting at 1:00 pm

    a. Collect the bags of food from the front porches of each of your 3 Block Captains.

    b. Count the bags and enter the count on the Bag Count Form, a copy of which is attached, and then feel free to consolidate the bags if it makes sense.

c. Deliver the bags of food to the food bank, starting at 1:00 pm. We anticipate everything being completed by 4:00 pm.

d. We will be on call to assist in any questions or issues.

5. On Sunday, May 5, after 1:00 pm pick up any straggler bags of food from the front porches of your Block Captains and deliver them to ______________.

6. Once we have completed our tallies, we will let you know the results of our collection effort.

If you have any questions or run into any issues, please call ________.

Many thanks for your efforts. This is one small way we can all make a difference.

Food Drive Committee

(Add member names and contact information)

Preparing Block Captain Packages

It is most convenient to have the bags, printed Food Drive Flyer & Neighbor Instructions, and other materials delivered to a central location, typically to a volunteer's home, to prepare the Bag Packages for the Collection Coordinators to deliver to the Block Captains. There should be enough room to layout a Block Captain Bag Package for each Block Captain around the assembly area.

The Block Captain Packages include:

- The appropriate number of two-sided Food Drive Flyer & Neighbor Instructions (Documents 12 & 13) to distribute to assigned block homes

- The appropriate number of bags to distribute to assigned block homes
- One Block Assignment List of assigned addresses for that block unit (Document 11)
- One Block Captain Responsibilities (Document 14)

Preparing Collection Coordinator Packages

Collection Coordinator with be provided with:

- One Bag Count Form (Document 17)
- One Block Assignments List (Document 11)
- One Collection Coordinator Responsibilities (Document 18)
- A Block Captain Bag Package for each assigned Block Captain

---

— DOCUMENT 17 —
BAG COUNT FORM

Food Drive Bag Count Form

Thank you for your participation as a Collection Coordinator for the Neighborhood Food Drive! When collecting the bags from your three (3) assigned Block Captains, please start your pick-up at 1:00 pm sharp, so we can complete the delivery by 3:00 pm or earlier.

Also, please count the bags on each Block Captain's porch and fill in the number of bags below. Feel free to consolidated bags after the count if you wish.

Please turn in this form at the weigh-in table at the food bank.

COLLECTION COORDINATOR: ____________________

Block No. ____________

Block Captain Name:

____

Number of bags: ______

Block No. ____________

Block Captain Name:

____

Number of bags: ______

Block No. ____________

Block Captain Name:

____

Number of bags: ______

— DOCUMENT 18 —

COLLECTION COORDINATOR RESPONSIBILITIES

Collection Coordinator Responsibilities

A Collection Coordinator's main duties are delivering the appropriate number of grocery bags to their assigned Block Captains and retrieving the filled bags and delivering them to the food banks on the food drive day. More specifically:

- As a Collection Coordinator, you will be assigned from 3 to 6 Block Captains.
- You will pick-up your Block Captain Bag Packages (grocery bags, food driver flyers, assigned addresses) from the designated location.

- You will deliver a Block Captain Bag Package to each of your assigned Block Captains at least a week before the food drive date.
- On the food drive date, after 1:00 pm, you will pick up the bags of groceries from the porch of each of your assigned Block Captains and enter the number of bags on the Bag Count Form.
- You will deliver the bags of food to the designated food bank.
- You will deliver a completed Bag Count Form at the weigh-in table or to a food drive committee member at the food bank.
- On the day after the food drive date, you will pick up any straggler bags of groceries from the assigned Block Captains' front porches.
- You will deliver straggler bags to the designated location.
- If you also want to assist in unloading and delivery of the grocery bags at the food bank on the food drive date, your assistance is appreciated.

Though the assembly of the packages can be done by one person, it is much easier and more efficient to have several volunteers. In most places schools now require student public service hours. We have successfully recruited several neighborhood students to assist in the assembly of these packages to fulfill their public service requirement.

The first step is to print off the Block Assignment List, which as we previously indicated lists the block number, the number of bags needed (the same as the number of units in that block), the addresses assigned to that block, the Block Captain's name and address, and the Collection Coordinator's name. The Block Assignment List is then cut into slips, one for each block. These slips will provide the addresses for the particular block and will be attached to the Block Captain's Responsibilities sheet. Additional copies of the List will be needed to provide one copy to each Collection Coordinator.

A volunteer can take a Block Assignment slip and determine the number of units required for that specific block. The volunteer counts out the same number of bags and the same number of Food Drive Flyer & Neighbor Instructions and places the bags and flyers together in one pile. Depending on the number of volunteers, one may call out the number on the slip, while another counts the corresponding number of bags, and still another counts out the corresponding number of Food Drive Flyer & Neighbor Instructions. Use whatever method works for you. Attach the Block Assignment slip to a Block Captain Responsibilities sheet as a reminder of duties and place it on top of the bags and flyers for that Block Captain to complete the Bag Package. Then place a large sticky note on top with the Block Number and the Collection Coordinator's name for easy identification. This should be repeated until there is a completed Bag Package for each Block Captain.

To prepare for the Collection Coordinators to pick up their Bag Packages, we found it helpful to stack the 3 to 6 assigned Block Captain packages together in one stack for each Collection Coordinator, alternating horizontal and vertical for each Captain's Bag Package for easy separation and delivery. Finally, we add a Bag Count Form (Document 17) on top of each Collection Coordinator's stack and a copy of the Collection Coordinators Responsibilities (Document 18). The stacks are now ready for pick up.

A step-by-step Bag Package assembly procedure is provided in the appendix as a bonus document.

Collection Coordinator Block Captain Bag Package Pick-up

The Collection Coordinator Instructions email (Document 16) designates times for the Collection Coordinators to pick-up their assigned Block Captain Bag Packages from the identified central location and deliver them to their Block Captains' homes so that the Block Captains can distribute the packages to the assigned neighbors the weekend prior to the food drive. Sometimes, the Collection Coordinators need a reminder email or call to come and pick-up their assigned Block Captain packages. When they pick up their set of packages, we suggest they immediately deliver the Block Captain Bag Packages on their way home. The goal is for Block Captains to distribute the grocery bags to the assigned neighbors the weekend before or soon as possible prior to the food drive, so the neighbors will have sufficient time to fill the bags prior to the drive date. We also quickly review their instructions again with the Collection Coordinators at pick-up. Repetition works.

Block Captain Bag Delivery

Once the Block Captains receive the Bag Packages, they will review the Block Captain Responsibilities with the attached Block Assignment slip with their assigned addresses. They will then prepare the bags for distribution by filling in their name and address on the Neighbor Instructions side of the Food Drive Flyer and either taping or stapling the prepared flyer (with the instructions and the block captain's name and address facing outward) to each grocery bag. Most of us receive sheets of preprinted name and address stickers to be used as return addresses on our mail from charities throughout the year. These stickers can be used to easily put the Block Captain's name and address in the appropriate space, thereby saving time. Now the empty bags are ready for distribution!

The bags should be distributed the weekend prior to the food drive date to their assigned addresses. Many Block Captains will know most of their neighbors and may want to knock on the door to deliver the bags and explain the food drive procedure and just visit with their neighbors. However, this is not necessary. A Block

Captain need only deliver the bags by placing them in a conspicuous dry place near the front door.

Food Bank Volunteers

Throughout the food drive process, leadership should be in regular communication with the food bank(s). Our job is to collect and deliver the food to the food bank. The food bank's job is to receive the food and bring it into their facility. As such, they will need advance notice in order to recruit their own volunteers to move, catalogue, and shelve the food on the day of the food drive. Of course, the food drive volunteers and the food bank volunteers will all be working together as a team to successfully deliver, count, weigh, move, catalogue, and place the food into the food bank.

Neighborhood Email Announcing the Food Drive

If you have a way to email your neighbors, you might want to send a simple email (Document 19) announcing the upcoming neighborhood food drive and then a couple of days before the drive send a reminder email to neighbors and the food drive volunteers (Document 20).

— DOCUMENT 19 —

ANNOUNCEMENT OF NEIGHBORHOOD FOOD DRIVE EMAIL

Subject Line: A Neighborhood Food Drive Saturday, May 4, 2024

Dear Neighbors,

A committee of several of your neighbors is holding a Neighborhood Food Drive to benefit ______________. This is a worthy way as a neighborhood to help out those in need in our community, and the need for a Food Drive is as great as any time.

Here's how it will work:

The Food Drive will be Saturday, May 4

1. The prior weekend, you will receive an empty grocery bag from one of your neighbors who has agreed to serve as your Block Captain to coordinate the food collection.
2. There will be an attached sheet with suggestions for food to contribute and instructions to return the bag to your Block Captain's front porch on Saturday, May 4, before 1:00 pm. If you will be out of town, you can drop off your bag early to your Block Captain.
3. If for some reason you do not receive a grocery bag to fill, please call or email ________________ and we will see that you get one.

Thank you in advance for your participation in this event. This is one small way we can all help. With everyone doing a little, we can accomplish a lot. We will report back to you on our success!

Neighborhood Food Drive Committee

(add member names and contact information)

— DOCUMENT 20 —

Reminder Email to Everyone

Subject Line: A Neighborhood Food Drive Saturday, May 4, 2024

Reminder, our Neighborhood Food Drive is this Saturday, May 4. On that day, **BEFORE 1:00 pm**, please drop off your grocery bag of non-perishables on the porch of your Block Captain at the address noted on the sheet you received with your bag.

Between 1:00 pm and 3:00 pm on Saturday, May 4, the bags will be picked up from the Block Captains' porches and delivered to the food bank by our Collection Coordinators. We're looking for a big turnout in this time of need! Please contribute to this worthy cause.

If any of you have any questions about the Neighborhood Food Drive, please contact ___________ at _________.

We will fill you in on the success of the food drive as soon as we have the results. All of you who are participating, whether as a Collection Coordinator, a Block Captain, or a contributing neighbor, **THANK YOU!!!**

This is one way we can help. With everyone doing a little, we can accomplish a lot.

Neighborhood Food Drive Committee

(add member names and contact information)

The Reminder Email to Everyone

It doesn't hurt to send the reminder email (Document 20) to the volunteers as well to keep the food drive running smoothly. It does provide all the necessary information about the event. If you prefer, you could send a short reminder group email to the Collection Coordinators to remind them of the date to pick up and deliver the Block Captain Packages and another reminder email few days before the food drive day to pick up the grocery bags from their Block Captains' porches. Likewise, a short reminder group email could be sent to the Block Captains a few days before the empty bags are scheduled to be delivered to them and another a few days before the food drive day to remind them that the grocery bags will be delivered to and picked up from their porches.

— 11 —

DOCUMENTING THE METRICS OF YOUR FOOD DRIVE

WE WANTED SOME metrics to share the results of our food drive efforts and use those metrics to compare them with past and future food drives. Just as importantly, we wanted the volunteers, the neighbors, and the food banks to see the statistical results of their efforts.

Main Metrics

Here are the main metrics to consider sharing:

- Number of bags distributed (based on household assignments to blocks)
- Number of bags collected (based on the Bag Collection Form completed by the Collection Coordinators or the data from the weight spreadsheet data)
- Total weight of the food collected (calculated from the weight spreadsheet data)
- Average weight of the bags collected

- Heaviest bag

- The total weight converted to number of meals (Total weight divided by 1.2)

- Number of homes in the neighborhood (from your earlier calculations on creating the units within the neighborhood)

- Number of additional bags distributed upon request, if any

- Number and names of volunteers (from your volunteer list)

The main metrics we use are the number of bags distributed and collected, the weight of the food collected, the number of meals, the number of homes, and the number of volunteers. The latter two are easily obtainable from our neighborhood map and our volunteer recruitment list. The conversion for the number of meals is the total weight divided by 1.2. We knew from the neighborhood maps how many homes would get a grocery bag. We also knew that upon request, we would distribute additional bags, which could be added the initial number of homes.

To obtain the collected grocery bag count for each block, we were dependent on the Collection Coordinators to provide us with a bag count. This ended up being haphazard with some providing the bag count for each block as requested, some providing overall total of bags collected from their assigned blocks, and others simply forgetting to do either. Our alternative was to count the bags weighed at the food banks, which was a close approximation of the bags collected, but did not provide the number of collected bags from each block. To provide a remedy for the confusion over the bag count for each block, we came up with a simple Bag Count Form (Document 17) for the Collection Coordinators to complete as they pick up the grocery bags from the porches of each of their assigned Block Captains.

Bag Weight Form

Another major metric is weight. We weigh each bag of the food collected as it is delivered to the food bank. One experience we had in an earlier drive was using a large commercial scale at the food bank to weigh all the bags we delivered at one time. At that time, we knew the number of bags we delivered and divided that number into the total weight to get the average weight of each bag we delivered.

Individual bag weights can be hand recorded in a printed Bag Weight Form (Document 21—a simplified version) and input into a digital spreadsheet at a later date or the bag weights can be input directly into that digital Bag Weight Form.

— DOCUMENT 21 —

BAG WEIGHT FORM

UNIT 1	UNIT 2	UNIT 3	UNIT 4	UNIT 5	UNIT 6	UNIT 7	UNIT 8	UNIT 9	UNIT 10
32.2	7.6	15.7	12.9	6.4	32.3	26.8	26.7	10.5	14.6
11.5	27.6	23.8	24.6	19.8	19.9	25.6	12.6	19.8	29.2
28.3	33.4	13.6	18.5	20.4	26.4	27.3	19.7	32.9	18.9
15.4	16.2	26.3	12.2	17.6	17.6	12.6	33.2	27.3	23.7
18.9	34.1	31.9	19.8	23.1	24.1	29.1	21.6	25.1	24.3
28.9	26.6	25.2	28.2	16.8	19.3	31.3	18.6	18.7	31.5
32.1	19.4	16.5	30.1	29.8	17.6	15.8	27.1	27.8	30.1
TOTALS									
167.3	164.9	153	134.1	133.9	157.2	168.5	159.5	162.1	172.3
Total # bags				70					
Total weight				1,573					
Avg bag weight				22.47					
$ collected				$xxx					

Except for the numbers at the bottom of the spread sheet, the individual numbers represent the weight of each individual bag. The weight entries are not entered by blocks but rather simply entered as any given bag is brought to the table to be weighed to keep the process moving smoothly. The totals at the bottom of a column reflect the sum of that column. Since we do deliver to two different food banks, we have two different Bag Weight Forms that we later combine. In this case, we do segment the columns for the second food bank so that we know what was delivered to each bank. Then we create a grand total for them at the bottom of the spreadsheet. These numbers provided us with a number of interesting metrics:

- The total bag weight for each of the two food banks, separately and collectively
- The total average bag weight for each of the two food banks, separately and collectively
- The total number of meals using the conversion of the total weight divided by 1.2 for each of the two food banks, separately and collectively
- The total numbers of bags for each of the two food banks, separately and collectively
- The total amount of checks contributed to each of the two food banks, separately and collectively

We were then able to provide the neighborhood, the Block Captains, the Collection Coordinators, and the food banks all of our metrics in our thank you messages to them in our Neighbor & Volunteer Thank You & Metrics message (Document 22) and our Business Flyer with Metrics to post in neighborhood businesses (Document 23).

— DOCUMENT 22 —

Neighbor & Volunteer Thank You Metrics Email

Neighbors and Volunteers,

Thank you for reaching into your hearts and kitchen pantries (or grocery store, as the case may be) to contribute to the **NEIGHBORHOOD FOOD DRIVE** on May 4, 2024 and making it a huge success. With your assistance and participation, a number of families need not go hungry during these difficult times. The food bank truly appreciated our neighborhood contributions. This was certainly a worthy way to help those in need.

Here's the success of our **2024 FOOD DRIVE** by the numbers:

601 . . . . Bags distributed throughout the neighborhood
36 . . . . Block Captain volunteers (insert names)
13 . . . . Collection Coordinator volunteers (insert names)
10 . . . . Additional volunteers who helped count, collate, unload, weigh and deliver bags (insert names)
5 . . . . Young volunteers (insert names)
335 . . . . Bags collected
4,100 lbs. . . Food collected
$850.00 . . . Monetary collections
2 . . . . Participating food banks (insert names)
1 . . . . First food bank: 262 Bags & 3,242 lbs.
1 . . . . Second food bank: 73 Bags & 857 lbs.
32.2 lbs. . . . Heaviest bag
12.24 lbs. . . Average weight of a bag
4 . . . . Donors (insert names)
2 . . . . Co-Chairs (insert names)
1 . . . . And a partridge in a pear tree … nope, not really

Congratulations and thanks to all of you who participated to make the 2024 NEIGHBORHOOD FOOD DRIVE a huge success. We can be proud of our neighborhood!

Food Drive Committee

(add member names and contact information)

— DOCUMENT 23 —

Business Flyer with Metrics

Thank you all for contributing to the success of this year's Neighborhood food drive on May 4. With your assistance and participation, a number of families need not go hungry. ____________ truly appreciates our neighborhood contributions.

Here's the success by the numbers:

335 . . . . . . Bags collected
4100 lbs. . . Food collected
4,920 . . . . Meals collected (lbs. / 1.2 = meals)
2 . . . . Food bank/s (Insert name/s)
32.2 lbs.. . . Heaviest bag
12.24 lbs. . . Average weight of a bag
32 . . . . Most bags collected from a Block Captain
104. . . . . . . Block Captains, Collection Coordinators & volunteers (insert names)
11. . . . . Young volunteers (insert names)
11. . . . . Food pantry volunteers (insert names)
1 . . . . And one huuuuge success!

— 12 —

THE DAY OF THE FOOD DRIVE

THE DAY OF the food drive finally arrives! Rain or shine, it happens.

Neighbors' Bag Delivery

Through the Food Drive Flyer & Neighbor Instructions delivered with the bags, the neighbors know the type of food to contribute and when and where to deliver the bags of food. The bags are to be delivered back to the Block Captain's porch before 1:00 pm on the day of the food drive, so that the Collection Coordinators can begin the collection and delivery of the bags on the same day at 1:00 pm to deliver them to the food bank.

It is not essential that the Block Captains be present the day of the food drive, but it is helpful if they can assist the Collection Coordinators in loading up the vehicles that are delivering the food to the food banks. Though asked to deliver the day of the food drive, some eager beaver neighbors as well going-out-of-towners may deliver their bags a day or two before food drive day. This is typically not a problem. However, the Block Captains should protect the early bags from possible inclement weather.

Collection Coordinator Bag Pick-up & Delivery

After the 1:00 pm deadline for dropping off bags, the next work begins. All of the Collection Coordinators begin to pick-up the bags from the porches of their respective Block Captains at 1:00 pm. Those with SUVs, vans, or trucks may be able to pick-up all of the bags from all of their Block Captains in one trip. Others may have to make 2 or 3 trips. As they are loading the bags into their vehicles, the Collection Coordinators should count the bags retrieved from each Block Captain's porch and record the number on the Bag Count Form (Document 17) for each pickup. After the count, Collection Coordinators, at their discretion, may consolidate the bags to avoid ripped or damaged bags.

The Collection Coordinators will then take the bags to the designated food bank. Be mindful that the delivery point and the weighing process can be choke points if a number of Collection Coordinators arrive at collection drop off at the same time. Assigning Collection Coordinators specific drop off times may help alleviate congestion. This will not work perfectly as there will be early and late arrivals, but it might reduce some of the congestion.

Upon arrival, volunteers will assist in unloading the vehicles and delivering the bags for weighing and recording. Often the organizations have wagons or carts which can be used to move the bags from the vehicles to the weighing tables. You can request the Collection Coordinators either to drop off their Bag Count Form at the weigh-in table or give the form to an assigned onsite food drive leader. Unless the Collection Coordinators wish to assist in the unloading and moving grocery bags, their job is complete with the exception of picking up and dropping off straggler bags.

Food Bank Set-up

Prior to the day of the food drive, confirm with the food bank(s) that they are ready for the food drive and have their own volunteers ready for the delivery and shelving of the groceries. A scale or two should have been obtained by this point. The food drive leaders should be on site with other volunteers they recruit for the day of the food drive. It is best to set up at the food bank at least 30 minutes prior to the 1:00 pm delivery start.

The set-up should include a couple of folding tables and chairs near the drop-off point, a scale or two for weighing the bags, pens and Bag Weight Form (Document 21) for recording the bag weight or a laptop or tablet to enter this data directly into the form, a few wagons for carrying the bags from the drop off point to the weighing station and the weighing station to where the food will be shelved. Having bottled water in a cooler or coffee for the volunteers is also nice. Typically, the beneficiary will have folding tables and chairs that can be used, but confirm this ahead in case you need to bring your own.

Weighing the Bags

Set up the weight table(s) at the entrance to the food bank. We appreciated the generous loan of a commercial digital scale for the first two of our drives. The scale was a heavy, older digital model, but served its purpose. We now have two digital scales (costing under $50 each) that were donated to the cause. The scales have digital readers tethered to them, so the weight can easily be read even if the bags cover the entire scale. Though one scale is enough, two scales work the best to facilitate the weighing process. The two scales can be used simultaneously at a food bank to speed up recording the bag weights, or, if there is a secondary food bank participating, one scale can be assigned to each location.

As the Collection Coordinators arrive, volunteers should be ready to direct traffic. The drop off point will determine if traffic needs to be directed away from the drop off point so the unloading of the bags can be done safely. When necessary, orange traffic cones may be used to divert traffic from the drop off point.

Volunteers are also needed to unload the bags into wagons and move the bags to the weigh stations. Volunteers at the weight table will weigh and record the bag weights on the Bag Weight Form while other volunteers assist with the delivery of the bags into the food bank. Food drive volunteers should also clean-up the area after the work is done.

When several Collection Coordinators arrive at the food bank at the same time, the delivered bags may pile up at the entrance to the food bank, but by working efficiently in moving the bags and recording the weights, everything can be accomplished within the desired two or three hour allotted time. Using two scales will make weighing the bags more efficient. Having sufficient volunteers to help move the bags will be very helpful.

Completion

Typically, the actual food drive takes less than 3 hours from the 1:00 pm start time to the end of deliveries, including any site clean-up by those volunteers who stay the entire time. Most Collection Coordinators are finished in a short time. Not a big ask of any of the volunteers. The onsite leaders should collect all of the Bag Count Forms that the Collection Coordinators turn in and collect all of the bag weight recordings for the final metrics.

Publicity

Publicity is always good. You might have a volunteer assigned to take photos of the volunteers in action, especially the young volunteers, and obtain the names of all of the food drive volunteers as well as the food bank volunteers for future publicity in local papers and news. Articles can be written to send to the media and news outlets and can be submitted to local newsletters and news sites. Everyone loves recognition, and it serves as a basis for future recruitment if your food drive becomes an ongoing event.

In addition, the Business Flyer with Metrics (Document 23) that you create should be delivered to the neighborhood businesses with a request that they be posted on their premises.

— 13 —

COLLECTING STRAGGLER BAGS

STRAGGLER BAGS HAPPEN. As with the eager beavers, who drop off bags early, every neighborhood has some slow-pokes, who are late in dropping off the bags and miss the 1:00 pm deadline. It is not a huge issue, but it must be anticipated. The Block Captain Instructions ask the Block Captains let leadership know if anyone delivers bags late, so they can be picked up while the Food Drive is ongoing. In any case, any remaining straggler bags will be picked up on the following day by the Collection Coordinators.

Straggler Bags Pick-Up & Delivery

The Collection Coordinators should drive by their respective Block Captains' homes the day after the drive to see if there are any straggler bags on the porches. If so, they should be delivered to a designated central location in case the food bank is closed, which may be the case it the straggler pick-up day is a Sunday. All of the straggler bags can be delivered to the food bank the following business day by one of the volunteers or leaders.

— 14 —

THANK YOU, THANK YOU, THANK YOU

ONCE THE FOOD drive has been completed, it is time to thank all of the volunteers (Document 24), be they Block Captains, Collection Coordinators, donating neighbors, or other volunteers. You can never thank the volunteers enough. They make the food drive a success. Start by sending a short thank you email to all of the Block Captains, the Collection Coordinators, food drive volunteers and your food bank contact the same day as the food drive. Since you already have a group email for these groups, it is easy to do. A warm thank you message goes a long way. It not only provides an opportunity to thank the volunteers, it is an opportunity to seek comments for improvement from those on the front lines.

— DOCUMENT 24 —

Same-Day Thank You to Volunteers Email

Block Captains, Collection Coordinators, and Volunteers:

Thank you all for contributing to the success of this year's **NEIGHBORHOOD FOOD DRIVE**. With your assistance and participation, a number of families need not go hungry during these difficult times. The food bank truly appreciates our neighborhood contributions. They will go a long way in feeding the needy in our community.

Your efforts worked well. Bags were distributed, neighbors returned a high number of full grocery bags to the Block Captains, and Collection Coordinators picked up and delivered the bags to the food bank. The bags were counted and weighed, and we were able to complete the work in about 2 hours. We'll pick up any straggler bags tomorrow. We will send you the metrics for the food drive once we have everything tallied.

If you have any suggestions or comments to improve the food drive, please take the time to let us know.

Congratulations to all of you and thank you for participating in making the drive a huge success. You all can be proud of your efforts and our neighborhood. If you would like to serve on the Food Drive Committee for next year's food drive, please us know.

Take care and stay healthy!

Food Drive Committee

(add member names and contact information)

Thank You with Metrics

Earlier we discussed metrics. The volunteers appreciate knowing the results of their efforts. The metrics serve this purpose. Having counted, weighed, and recorded the bags, having a list of Collection Coordinators, Block Captains, donors, participating food banks, and other volunteers, we have a lot of metrics to share with all involved. Once the metrics are processed, another big thank you email can be sent to the volunteers, neighbors, and beneficiaries providing them with such metrics as the number of bags, the total weight, the average weight, the equivalent number of meals, the number of volunteers, the non-food donations and other interesting metrics that show the success of the food drive. It also allows comparison from year to year if you hold future drives. A thank you email with the metrics is shown in Document 22.

In addition, to thanking the volunteers, we also printed a flyer which carried the essential metrics quantifying the success and a thank you to the neighborhood. We distributed the flyer to the businesses in the area to post on their premises so neighbors and friends become aware of the food drive and its success. Document 23 is a sample of how to share metrics in a flyer.

— 15 —

PREPARING FOR CONTINUITY AND SUCCESSION

HAVING CONDUCTED OUR Neighborhood Food Drive now for several years, it has become a source of community action and accomplishment. We have it down to a science, so that it almost runs itself. The neighborhood looks forward to it and many individuals volunteer year after year. I don't know if this is because they are committed to the cause or because we have made it so easy that they cannot refuse. Nonetheless, we recognize that if the annual event is to continue there must be some continuity and a means of succession.

We established an ongoing food drive committee to provide the needed continuity and a means of leadership succession. Though we have been able to run food drives with just two committee members, we now have a committee of six committed neighbors, who will be involved in the intricacies of the food drive and the planning of the future food drives. We have also documented our own food drive process through a slimmed down version of this book, so new leadership will not have to re-create the wheel. They will be able to rely on the experience and history of the prior food drives.

— 16 —

CONCLUSION

OUR MANTRA HAS been "If everyone does a little, we can accomplish a lot." A neighborhood food drive is driven by volunteers, without whom there would be no food drive. Keeping each volunteer's duties to a minimum is a key. Each volunteer only does a little. Block Captains deliver bags to a small group of neighbors and allow their porch to be a drop off point. Collection Coordinators drop off a package of bags to each of their Block Captains and pick up and deliver the filled bags to the food banks. Neighbors fill a grocery bag and drop it off at their Block Captain's porch. Designated food banks provide volunteers to receive the food. No one does very much, but together we have made a difference.

I hope this book encourages you to take the leap and gives you the courage, confidence, and tools to organize your first neighborhood food drive. I wish you the best in your endeavor!

APPENDIX

— DOCUMENT 1 —

Kick-Off Email to Food Bank & Donors

Subject: May 4 Food Drive

All,

We just wanted to let you know we have kicked off our 2024 Food Drive scheduled for May 4 by sending out our Block Captain Recruitment Letter and reaching out to Collection Coordinator volunteers. The recruitment letter below explains the timing and the nuts and bolts of the food drive. We expect to begin bringing the bags of groceries to the food pantry after 1:00 pm on May 4. We expect the process of delivery, weighing, and receiving the groceries to take no more than two to three hours.

Thank you to those who are donating supplies for the drive. We sincerely appreciate your willingness to do this.

Thanks to all of you for your help and support. If you have any questions, please do not hesitate to call _____________.

Food Drive Committee

— DOCUMENT 2 —
Neighborhood Map

— DOCUMENT 3 —

Block Captain Recruitment Email

Subject: Request for volunteers for Neighborhood Food Drive

Several of us in the neighborhood are spearheading a Neighborhood Food Drive to help address the needs of the hungry and food insecure in our community. Food insecurity in the United States increased by 6% in 2023. It is reported that 47.4 million people—1 in 7 people, including 1 in 5 children—experience food insecurity in the US. Even here in our community there is food insecurity. We will be collecting food for a local food bank to help them achieve their mission of meeting the needs of the hungry in our community. **A local food drive is about making a difference by engaging a community to collectively take action in a way that most certainly will make a real, personal difference in lives.** We are asking you to be a Block Captain for the Neighborhood Food Drive Campaign. It will be so easy to participate.

Here's how:

The Neighborhood Food Drive is Saturday, May 4, 2024

1. You will be assigned to represent about 10 to 15 houses on your block area.
2. **Around April 27**, you will receive a package of empty grocery bags from one of your neighbors, who has agreed to assist in the coordination of the food collection. You will receive flyers with suggestions for food to contribute and instructions on returning the bags full of groceries to your front porch on **Saturday, May 4 before 1:00 pm.** Finally, you will receive a list of addresses on or around your home for grocery bag distribution.
3. As soon as possible after receipt of the grocery bags and the flyers, **print your name and address on the flyer so neighbors will know where to drop off their groceries.** Staple or tape a flyer to the outside of each grocery bag so your name is showing. Then the bags should be

distributed right away to your neighbors *at the addresses assigned to you.*

4. **On Saturday, May 4, before 1:00 pm**, your assigned neighbors will drop off their filled grocery bags to your front porch. You need not be present. If there are any straggler bags, please call your Collection Coordinator ASAP so they can be picked up during the Food Drive. Otherwise, they will be picked up on Sunday, **May 5.**
5. **On Saturday, May 4, after 1:00 pm,** your Collection Coordinator will pick up the grocery bags from your front porch and take them to the food bank. You need not be present.
6. On **Sunday, May 5, after 1:00 pm**, your Collection Coordinator will pick up from your front porch any grocery bags from any stragglers who missed the deadline and take them to the designated location. You need not be present.
7. If you also want to assist in the loading, unloading and delivery of the grocery bags for the food bank, we certainly could use the assistance to make this food drive a success.

With everyone doing a little, we will accomplish a lot. **Please confirm by return email (with your telephone number and address) that you will be a Food Drive Block Captain**. This is one small way we can all help.

If for any reason you will be unable to serve as a Block Captain, would you please help us find your replacement by quickly recruiting a neighbor on your block and let us know the individual's contact information? Many thanks for your consideration.

Food Drive Committee

(add committee names and contact information)

— DOCUMENT 4 —

Block Captain Confirmation Email

Subject: Thank you for volunteering to help with the Neighborhood Food Drive

Thank you so much for volunteering to be a Block Captain for the 2024 Neighborhood Food Drive. With your help, we can do a lot to help out those who are in need.

You will receive the grocery bags along with a two-side event flyer & instructions for the homes on your assigned block about a week before the Saturday, May 4 Food Drive Day. You will need to put your name and address on the instruction side of the flyer, attach that flyer to each bag (instruction side facing out) and then deliver the bags to the homes on your assigned block. If you have any homes on your block that are not listed, please deliver bags to the unlisted homes and let us know the addresses so we can add them to the list for future drives.

On Saturday, May 4, the neighbors on your block will return the filled grocery bags to your front porch (covered area in the event of inclement weather) by 1:00 pm and soon thereafter the Collection Coordinators will come by and pick up all the bags. If neighbors drop off bags late, let your Collection Coordinator know, and the bags will either be picked up later on drive day or the next day.

Again, thanks so much for volunteering!

Food Drive Committee

(Add member names and contact information)

— DOCUMENT 5 —

Block Captain Regrets Email

Subject: Thank you for volunteering to help with the Neighborhood Food Drive

Thank you so much for volunteering to be a Block Captain for the 2024 Neighborhood Food Drive. With your help, we can do a lot to help out those who are in need.

You will receive the grocery bags along with a two-side event flyer & instructions for the homes on your assigned block about a week before the Saturday, May 4 Food Drive Day. You will need to put your name and address on the instruction side of the flyer, attach that flyer to each bag (instruction side facing out) and then deliver the bags to the homes on your assigned block. If you have any homes on your block that are not listed, please deliver bags to the unlisted homes and let us know the addresses so we can add them to the list for future drives.

On Saturday, May 4, the neighbors on your block will return the filled grocery bags to your front porch (covered area in the event of inclement weather) by 1:00 pm and soon thereafter the Collection Coordinators will come by and pick up all the bags. If after pick-up, neighbors drop off bags late, let your Collection Coordinator know, and the bags will either be picked up drive day or the next day.

Again, thanks so much for volunteering!

Food Drive Committee

(Add member names and contact information)

— DOCUMENT 6 —

Collection Coordinator Recruitment Email

Subject: Request for volunteers for Neighborhood Food Drive

The Neighborhood Food Drive Committee is spearheading a Neighborhood Food Drive to help address the needs of the hungry and food insecure in our community. Food insecurity in the United States increased by 6% in 2023. It is reported that 47.4 million people—1 in 7 people, including 1 in 5 children—experience food insecurity in the US. Even here in our community. We will be collecting food for a local food bank to help them achieve their mission of meeting the needs of the hungry in our community. **A local food drive is about making a difference by engaging a community to collectively take action in a way that most certainly will make a real, personal difference in lives.**

We are asking you to be a Collection Coordinator for this Neighborhood Food Drive on **Saturday, May 4**. It will be so easy to participate.

As a Coordinator, you will be assigned a small number of volunteer Block Captains. We intend and expect to have 48 Block Captains, and you will likely be the coordinator for 3 of them. The Committee is in the process of signing up the Block Captains. Once this is accomplished, we will let you know which ones would be assigned to you.

We will be sending you more details for your role in the food drive shortly, but simply, your duties will be:

1. Picking up a set of grocery bags and flyers with instructions for each of your Block Captains from a designated location between **April 25-27** from 10:00 am - 6:00 pm
2. Delivering the grocery bags and flyers with instructions to each of your Block Captains
3. Responding to any questions from the Block Captains or referring them to a Food Drive Committee member

— DOCUMENT 6 (cont'd) —

4. On Saturday, **May 4**, beginning at 1:00 pm, picking up the bags of food from the front porch of each of your Block Captains
5. Counting the bags for each Block Captain and entering the count on the Bag Count Form
6. Delivering the bags of food to the designated Food Bank
7. On Sunday **May 5**, picking up any straggler bags of food from each of your Block Captains' front porches
8. Delivering straggler bags to designated collection point

With everyone doing a little, we will accomplish a lot. **Please confirm by return email (with your telephone number and address) if you will be a Neighborhood Food Drive Collection Coordinator this year.**

If for any reason, you will be unable to serve as a Collection Coordinator, as time is of the essence, please help us find your replacement by recruiting a neighbor and letting us know the individual's contact information or simply share a name and we will make the contact.

Many thanks for your consideration. This is one small way we can all help.

In the meantime, if you have questions, feel free to reach out to us.

Neighborhood Food Drive Committee

(add committee names and contact information)

— DOCUMENT 7 —

Collection Coordinator Confirmation Email

Subject: Thank you for volunteering to help with the Neighborhood Food Drive

Thank you so much for volunteering to be a Collection Coordinator for the 2024 Neighborhood Food Drive. With your help we can do a lot to help out those who are in need.

You will be able to pick up sets of bags and flyers to deliver to your Block Captains on ____________ between __________ at _____________. We ask that the set of bags and flyers be delivered to your Block Captains as soon as possible so they can be distributed timely to the homes on their respective blocks. Then on May 4 starting at 1:00 pm, please pick up the filled bags from the porch of each of your Block Captains and deliver them to our designated food bank. On May 5, please check the porches of your Block Captains again to see if there are any straggler bags and, if so, deliver them to the designated location.

Again, thanks so much for volunteering!

Food Drive Committee

(Add member names and contact information)

— DOCUMENT 8 —

Collection Coordinator Regrets Email

Subject: May we ask for your help?

Thank you for your response. We are sorry, as we know you are, that you will be unable to volunteer as Collection Coordinator for our Neighborhood Food Drive.

Is it possible for you to recruit one of your neighbors to be a Collection Coordinator or can you suggest someone in the neighborhood that we might approach to be a Collection Coordinator? Since time is important, please let us know at your earliest convenience.

Thanks for your consideration and your continued support of this project.

Food Drive Committee

(Add member names and contact information)

— DOCUMENT 9 —

Block Captain Contacts Format

NAME	CONTACT INFO	PHONE
John Q. Public	johnq@gmail.com HOME: 1234 Main Street Sometown, NC 99999 WORK: Block 12 - Yes	919-999-9999 (cell)

— DOCUMENT 10 —

Collection Coordinator Contacts Format

NAME	CONTACT INFO	PHONE
John Q. Public	johnq@gmail.com HOME: 1234 Main Street Sometown, NC 99999 WORK: Block 12 - Smith Block 15 - Jones Block 16 - Brown	919-999-9999 (cell)

— DOCUMENT 11 —

Block Assignment List

Block 1 = 16 Bags **Smith** (Collection Coordinator)

Jones (Block Captain) 2113 Cherry St
Block Addresses:
Cherry Street — 2101, 2105, 2107, 2109, 2111, 2113, 2115, 2117, 2123, 2201, 2203, 2207, 2213
Elm Street — 2506, 2508, 2510

Block 2 = 18 Bags **Brown**

Green 2118 Glen St
Block Addresses:
Glen St — 2014, 2108, 2110, 2114, 2116, 2118, 2202, 2204, 2206, 2208, 2210, 2211, 2212, 2214, 2216
Meadow Rd — 2406, 2408, 2410

Block 3 = 14 Bags **Black**

Adams 2130 Washington Dr
Block Addresses:
Washington Dr — 2127, 2128, 2129, 2130, 2131, 2132, 2133, 2134, 2135, 2137, 2139, 2141, 2020, 2022

— DOCUMENT 12 —

Food Drive Flyer

Who, What, When, Where, Why

A number of us in the neighborhood have recognized the need for a food drive to help out the hungry and food insecure of our community, so the neighborhood is holding a **Neighborhood Food Drive**, and we hope you will support it.

The groceries collected will benefit ____________.

- **Around April 27**, a week before the **May 4** Neighborhood Food Drive, you will receive an empty grocery bag on your doorstep from your neighborhood Food Drive Block Captain with suggestions for items needed by the food bank benefiting from the food drive.
- Please return the bag with the food items to your Block Captain's porch no later than **1:00 pm on May 4**.
- Our goal is to raise over 4,000 pounds of food to help feed the hungry in our area. We hope you will support this project in any way you can.
- **For more information contact:** Food Drive Committee. Email, telephone number

— ***See reverse for more Food Drive information!*** —

— DOCUMENT 13 —

Neighbor Instructions

Neighborhood Food Drive May 4, 2024

Thank you for your participation in the Neighborhood Food Drive! Please return the bag to your Block Captain by **1:00 pm, Saturday, May 4**. If you will be out of town for the weekend, you can return your bag early to your Block Captain.

Your Block Captain is: ______________________________

Address: ______________________________________

Most Wanted Food & Grocery Items

- No glass
- Canned pasta with meat (example: ravioli w/ meatballs)
- Beef stew and healthy soups
- Cereal/granola/oatmeal & other breakfast items (all sizes)
- Chicken or tuna (cans or pouches), salmon
- Canned chili with beans and/or black beans
- Mac & cheese (cups or boxes)
- Cliff bars, kind bars, or granola bars
- Individual fruit cups or canned fruit
- Individual vegetable cups or canned vegetables, beans & tomatoes
- Juice boxes
- Sandwich crackers
- Peanut butter and jelly
- Pasta and rice
- Dried peas, beans

— ***See reverse for more Food Drive information!*** —

— DOCUMENT 14 —

Block Captain Responsibilities

Block Captain Responsibilities

A Block Captain's main duties are delivering the grocery bags with the Food Drive Flyer & Neighbor Instructions and having the neighbors return the grocery bags to their front porch. More specifically:

- A Block Captain will be assigned 10 to 15 houses in Block Captain's block.
- At least a week prior to the food drive date, a package of empty grocery bags will be delivered to the Block Captain's home along with Food Drive Flyer & Neighbor Instructions and a list of assigned addresses near the Block Captain's address.
- Upon receipt, the each flyer should be filled in with the Block Captain's name and address and attached to the outside of a grocery bag, the instruction side facing outward.
- As soon after bag receipt and preparation as possible, the bags should be distributed to the assigned addresses.
- On the food drive date, before 1:00 pm, your assigned neighbors will drop off their full grocery bags to your front porch. You need not be present.
- On the food drive date, after 1:00 pm, the grocery bags will be picked up from your front porch and taken to the food bank. You need not be present.
- The day after the food drive date, after 1:00 pm, any straggler bags that missed the deadline will be picked up and delivered to the designated location. You need not be present.
- If you want to assist in the loading, unloading and delivery of the grocery bags to the food bank, your assistance would be appreciated.

— DOCUMENT 15 —

Block Captain Instructions Email

Block Captains!

We have been planning, preparing, and recruiting for the 2024 NEIGHBORHOOD FOOD DRIVE, and we are so thankful for all of you who have volunteered to be a Block Captain. The Food Drive is a worthy way to help those in need.

All of the 2024 planning is complete, and now it's time to execute. Here is your action plan for the Saturday, May 4 Food Drive.

1. During the early part of the weekend of April 27, the Collection Coordinators will drop off at your house sufficient grocery bags (12 to 20) for the assigned houses on your block unit.
2. You will also receive 2-sided flyers with suggestions for food to contribute and instructions on returning the grocery bags to your front porch on Saturday, May 4, before 1:00 pm. A copy of the 2-sided flyer is attached.
3. Last but not least, the Block Assignment List of assigned addresses is attached. Look for your name on the list. Block Captain's name and address are listed in BOLD on the left-hand side under the Block Number. The Collection Coordinator's name is listed in BOLD on the middle across from the Block Number. Look closely at your assigned addresses, which do not necessarily coincide with your own block.
4. Upon receipt, please fill in your name and address on the Neighbor Instructions side of the flyer (Hint: Use the freebie address labels you regularly receive from charitable organizations). The flyer should be stapled or taped to the outside of each grocery bag with your name and address showing outward.
5. Early in the week prior to the food drive, distribute the bags to your neighbors *at the addresses assigned* to you to give them enough time to fill the bags with groceries. Let us know if you need more bags or if there are any omitted

— DOCUMENT 15 (cont'd) —

addresses on your block area so we can add them to the list. Look closely at your assigned addresses, which do not necessarily coincide with your exact block.

6. On Saturday, May 4, before 1:00 pm, your assigned neighbors will drop off their full grocery bags on your front porch. You need not be present. If you will have a drop off point other than your front porch, let us know so we will know where to pick up the groceries. We will urge your neighbors to deliver the groceries where possible on the morning of Saturday, May 4. Rain or shine, it will be Saturday, May 4. Please try to protect the bags from the elements in case of inclement weather.
7. On Saturday, May 4 after 1:00 pm, Collection Coordinators will pick up the grocery bags from your front porch and take them to the food bank. You need not be present. Let your Collection Coordinator know ASAP if anyone delivers bags late, so they can be picked up while the food drive is ongoing if possible.
8. On Sunday, May 5, after 1:00 pm, your Collection Coordinator will pick up any straggler bags that missed the deadline and take them to the designated location. You need not be present.
9. If you want to assist in the loading, delivery, and unloading of the grocery bags, we certainly could use the assistance to make this food drive a success.
10. Once we get everything tallied, we will let you know the results of our collection effort.

If you have any questions or run into any issues, please call __________.

Many thanks for your efforts. This is one small way we can all make a difference.

Food Drive Committee

(Add member names and contact information)

— DOCUMENT 16 —

Collection Coordinator Instructions Email

Collection Coordinators!

We have been planning, preparing, and recruiting for the 2024 NEIGHBORHOOD FOOD DRIVE, and we are so thankful for all of you who have volunteered to be a Collection Coordinator. The Food Drive is a worthy way to help out those in need.

All of the food drive planning is done and now it's time to execute. Here is your action plan for the Saturday, May 4 Food Drive.

1. Each of the Collection Coordinators will be assigned 3 Block Captains to whom you will deliver bags and pick up groceries. Your Assigned Block Captains are on the attached Block Assignment List.
2. Between April 25-27, 10:00 am to 6:00 pm, please pick up the assigned Bag Packages with grocery bags, flyers, and a list of assigned addresses for your Block Captains at ___________. Please call or email (999-999-9999 or ___________@gmail.com) to let us know the approximate time you will pick up your three sets of bags or if there are any issues in picking up the bags.
3. As soon as possible after pick-up but in any event by April 27, deliver the appropriate grocery bags, flyers, and list of assigned addresses to your Block Captains and respond to any questions they may have.
4. On Saturday, Saturday, May 4 starting at 1:00 pm
    a. Collect the bags of food from the front porches of each of your 3 Block Captains.
    b. Count the bags and enter the count on the Bag Count Form, a copy of which is attached, and then feel free to consolidate the bags if it makes sense.

— DOCUMENT 16 (cont'd) —

  c. Deliver the bags of food to the food bank, starting at 1:00 pm. We anticipate everything being completed by 4:00 pm.

  d. We will be on call to assist in any questions or issues.

5. On Sunday, May 5, after 1:00 pm pick up any straggler bags of food from the front porches of your Block Captains and deliver them to ________________.

6. Once we have completed our tallies, we will let you know the results of our collection effort.

If you have any questions or run into any issues, please call ________.

Many thanks for your efforts. This is one small way we can all make a difference.

Food Drive Committee

(Add member names and contact information)

— DOCUMENT 17 —
Bag Count Form

Food Drive Bag Count Form

Thank you for your participation as a Collection Coordinator for the Neighborhood Food Drive! When collecting the bags from your three (3) assigned Block Captains, please start your pick-up at 1:00 pm sharp, so we can complete the delivery by 3:00 pm or earlier. Also, please count the bags on each Block Captain's porch and fill in the number of bags below. Feel free to consolidated bags after the count if you wish.

Please turn in this form at the weigh-in table at the food bank.

COLLECTION COORDINATOR: ______________________

Block No. ____________
Block Captain Name:

____

Number of bags: _______

Block No. ____________
Block Captain Name:

____

Number of bags: _______

Block No. ____________
Block Captain Name:

____

Number of bags: _______

— DOCUMENT 18 —

Collection Coordinator Responsibilities

Collection Coordinator Responsibilities

A Collection Coordinator's main duties are delivering the appropriate number of grocery bags to their assigned Block Captains and retrieving the filled bags and delivering them to the food banks on the food drive day. More specifically:

- As a Collection Coordinator, you will be assigned from 3 to 6 Block Captains.
- You will pick-up your Block Captain Bag Packages (grocery bags, food driver flyers, assigned addresses) from the designated location.
- You will deliver a Block Captain Bag Package to each of your assigned Block Captains at least a week before the food drive date.
- On the food drive date, after 1:00 pm, you will pick up the bags of groceries from the porch of each of your assigned Block Captains and enter the number of bags on the Bag Count Form.
- You will deliver the bags of food to the designated food bank.
- You will deliver a completed Bag Count Form at the weigh-in table or to a food drive committee member at the food bank.
- On the day after the food drive date, you will pick up any straggler bags of groceries from the assigned Block Captains' front porches.
- You will deliver straggler bags to the designated location.
- If you also want to assist in unloading and delivery of the grocery bags at the food bank on the food drive date, your assistance is appreciated.

— DOCUMENT 19 —

Announcement of Neighborhood Food Drive Email

Subject Line: A Neighborhood Food Drive Saturday, May 4, 2024

Dear Neighbors,

A committee of several of your neighbors is holding a Neighborhood Food Drive to benefit ________________. This is a worthy way as a neighborhood to help out those in need in our community, and the need for a Food Drive is as great as any time.

Here's how it will work:

The Food Drive will be Saturday, May 4

1. The prior weekend, you will receive an empty grocery bag from one of your neighbors who has agreed to serve as your Block Captain to coordinate the food collection.
2. There will be an attached sheet with suggestions for food to contribute and instructions to return the bag to your Block Captain's front porch on Saturday, May 4, before 1:00 pm. If you will be out of town, you can drop off your bag early to your Block Captain.
3. If for some reason you do not receive a grocery bag to fill, please call or email __________________ and we will see that you get one.

Thank you in advance for your participation in this event. This is one small way we can all help. With everyone doing a little, we can accomplish a lot. We will report back to you on our success!

Neighborhood Food Drive Committee

(add member names and contact information)

— DOCUMENT 20 —

Reminder Email to Everyone

Subject Line: A Neighborhood Food Drive Saturday, May 4, 2024

Reminder, our Neighborhood Food Drive is this Saturday, May 4. On that day, **BEFORE 1:00 pm**, please drop off your grocery bag of non-perishables on the porch of your Block Captain at the address noted on the sheet you received with your bag.

Between 1:00 pm and 3:00 pm on Saturday, May 4 the bags will be picked up from the Block Captains' porches and delivered to the food bank by our Collection Coordinators. We're looking for a big turnout in this time of need! Please contribute to this worthy cause.

If any of you have any questions about the Neighborhood Food Drive, please contact ___________ at _________.

We will fill you in on the success of the food drive as soon as we have the results. All of you who are participating, whether as a Collection Coordinator, a Block Captain, or a contributing neighbor, **THANK YOU!!!**

This is one way we can help. With everyone doing a little, we can accomplish a lot.

Neighborhood Food Drive Committee

(add member names and contact information)

— DOCUMENT 21 —

Bag Weight Form

UNIT 1	UNIT 2	UNIT 3	UNIT 4	UNIT 5	UNIT 6	UNIT 7	UNIT 8	UNIT 9	UNIT 10
32.2	7.6	15.7	12.9	6.4	32.3	26.8	26.7	10.5	14.6
11.5	27.6	23.8	24.6	19.8	19.9	25.6	12.6	19.8	29.2
28.3	33.4	13.6	18.5	20.4	26.4	27.3	19.7	32.9	18.9
15.4	16.2	26.3	12.2	17.6	17.6	12.6	33.2	27.3	23.7
18.9	34.1	31.9	19.8	23.1	24.1	29.1	21.6	25.1	24.3
28.9	26.6	25.2	28.2	16.8	19.3	31.3	18.6	18.7	31.5
32.1	19.4	16.5	30.1	29.8	17.6	15.8	27.1	27.8	30.1
TOTALS									
167.3	164.9	153	134.1	133.9	157.2	168.5	159.5	162.1	172.3
Total # bags				70					
Total weight				1,573					
Avg bag weight				22.47					
$ collected				$xxx					

— DOCUMENT 22 —

Neighbor & Volunteer Thank You Metrics Email

Neighbors and Volunteers,

Thank you for reaching into your hearts and kitchen pantries (or grocery store, as the case may be) to contribute to the **NEIGHBORHOOD FOOD DRIVE** on May 4, 2024 and making it a huge success. With your assistance and participation, a number of families need not go hungry during these difficult times. The food bank truly appreciated our neighborhood contributions. This was certainly a worthy way to help those in need.

Here's the success of our **2024 FOOD DRIVE** by the numbe**rs:**

601 . . . . Bags distributed throughout the neighborhood
36 . . . . Block Captain volunteers (insert names)
13 . . . . Collection Coordinator volunteers (insert names)
10 . . . . Additional volunteers who helped count, collate, unload, weigh and deliver bags (insert names)
5 . . . . Young volunteers (insert names)
335 . . . . Bags collected
4,100 lbs. . . Food collected
$850.00 . . . Monetary collections
2 . . . . Participating food banks (insert names)
1 . . . . First food bank: 262 Bags & 3,242 lbs.
1 . . . . Second food bank: 73 Bags & 857 lbs.
32.2 lbs. . . . Heaviest bag
12.24 lbs. . . Average weight of a bag
4 . . . . Donors (insert names)
2 . . . . Co-Chairs (insert names)
1 . . . . And a partridge in a pear tree … nope, not really

Congratulations and thanks to all of you who participated to make the 2024 NEIGHBORHOOD FOOD DRIVE a huge success. We can be proud of our neighborhood!

Food Drive Committee

(add member names and contact information)

— DOCUMENT 23 —

Business Flyer with Metrics

Thank you all for contributing to the success of this year's Neighborhood food drive on May 4. With your assistance and participation, a number of families need not go hungry. ______________ truly appreciates our neighborhood contributions.

Here's the success by the numbers:

335 . . . . . . Bags collected
4100 lbs. . . Food collected
4,920 . . . . Meals collected (lbs. / 1.2 = meals)
2 . . . . Food bank/s (Insert name/s)
32.2 lbs.. . . Heaviest bag
12.24 lbs.. . Average weight of a bag
32 . . . . Most bags collected from a Block Captain
104 . . . . . . Block Captains, Collection Coordinators & volunteers (insert names)
11. . . . . Young volunteers (insert names)
11. . . . . Food pantry volunteers (insert names)
1 . . . . And one huuuuge success!

— DOCUMENT 24 —

Same-Day Thank You to Volunteers Email

Block Captains, Collection Coordinators, and Volunteers:

Thank you all for contributing to the success of this year's **NEIGHBORHOOD FOOD DRIVE**. With your assistance and participation, a number of families need not go hungry during these difficult times. The food bank truly appreciates our neighborhood contributions. They will go a long way in feeding the needy in our community.

Your efforts worked well. Bags were distributed, neighbors returned a high number of full grocery bags to the Block Captains, and Collection Coordinators picked up and delivered the bags to the food bank. The bags were counted and weighed, and we were able to complete the work in an about 2 hours. We'll pick up any straggler bags tomorrow. We will send you the metrics for the food drive once we have everything tallied.

If you have any suggestions or comments to improve food drive, please take the time to let us know.

Congratulations to all of you and thank you for participating in making the drive a huge success. You all can be proud of your efforts and our neighborhood. If you would like to serve on the Food Drive Committee for next year's food drive, please us know.

Take care and stay healthy!

Food Drive Committee

(add member names and contact information)

BONUS DOCUMENT

Preparing Block Captain Bag Packages

Before starting this project, you should have on hand your supply of grocery bags. You also should have the following printed materials ready:

- Sufficient two-sided Food Drive Flyer & Neighbor Instructions sheets so there is one for each bag plus spares
- Sufficient copies of the Block Captain Responsibilities for each Captain to receive one and a few spares (Printing this on a different color paper than the Food Drive Flyer is a good idea.)
- Sufficent copies of Collection Coordinator Responsibilities for each Coordinator to receive one
- Sufficient Bag Count Forms for each Collection Coordinator to receive one
- Sufficient copies of the up-to-date Block Assignment List so that one can be cut into strips so that each Block Captain can receive a slip for his or her block and a whole list can be provided to each Collection Coordinator

The Block Captain Bag Packages will consist of the following for each Block Captain:

- The number of bags corresponding to the number of addresses on the Block Assignment slip plus 3 additional spare bags
- The number of two-sided Food Drive Flyer with Neighbor Instructions equal to the number of grocery bags plus spares
- The one-sided Block Captain Responsibilities sheet
- The Block Assignment slip stapled to the Block Captain Responsibilities
- A yellow sticky with the block number on it for easy identification.

The Collection Coordinator Packages will consist of:

- Their assigned Block Captain Bag Packages
- The Block Assignment List showing the Block Captains for each Collection Coordinator
- One Bag Count Form
- One Collection Coordinator Responsibilities sheet

BONUS DOCUMENT (cont'd)

Assembling Block Captain Bag Packages

We found this a helpful process to assemble the Block Captain Bag Packages:

- Split the volunteers into teams of two—one to count the number of flyers noted on the Block Assignment slip for that Block Captain and the other to count the same number of grocery bags
- Stack the flyers on top of the bags
- Attach the Block Assignment slip for that Captain to a Block Captain Responsibilities sheet and place the sheet on top of the flyers
- Place a sticky note with the block number written large on it on top of the pile

Assembling Collection Coordinator Block Captain Packages

After the Block Captain packages are assembled and laid out for every Block Captain, the next step is to gather the correct Block Captain Packages for each Collection Coordinator. We found this process helpful:

- Call out the blocks for each Collection Coordinator for a volunteer to group the Collection Coordinator's Block Captain Bag Packages together
- Stack Bag Packages alternating vertical and horizontal to separate each Captain's package
- Place a Bag Count Form on top of the Collection Coordinator Package
- Place a copy of the Block Assignments List showing the Block Captains assigned to each Collection Coordinator on top of the Bag Count Form
- Add the Collection Coordinator Responsibilities sheet on top of the Bag Count Form
- Add a sticky note with the name of the Collection Coordinator on top of everything

The packages are now ready for the Collection Coordinators to come and pick them up.

ABOUT THE AUTHOR

WILLIAM HARAZIN has participated in, organized, and helped carry out successful annual food drives in his neighborhood since 2018. He has a passion for helping those in need. He is a lawyer, teacher, certified BBQ judge, and now a published author. As a lawyer in his own firm, he practices in the area of international law. As an Associate Professor, now retired, at North Carolina State University's Wilson College of Textiles, he taught international and law classes. In 2017, he was the recipient of the NASBITE International's International Trade Educator of the Year Award. Over his career, Bill has been involved in the international trade community holding leadership roles in many international organizations. He speaks regularly on international trade issues, giving him the opportunity to travel the world.

Bill grew up in Illinois and went to schools in the Midwest before moving to North Carolina with his wife, Becky. They both enjoy spending time at the North Carolina beaches and mountains when not traveling.

Made in the USA
Monee, IL
01 April 2025

15020993R00069